WORLD WAR II
AERONAUTICAL
RESEARCH
.... *at* ....
LANGLEY

WORLD WAR II
AERONAUTICAL RESEARCH
at
LANGLEY

MARK A. CHAMBERS

THE
History
PRESS

Published by The History Press
Charleston, SC
www.historypress.com

Front cover, top left: NASA Langley Research Center via Larry Loftin Collection.
Back cover, bottom: NASA Langley Research Center via Larry Loftin Collection.

Unless otherwise noted, all images are courtesy of NASA Langley Research Center.

First published 2022

Manufactured in the United States

ISBN 9781467149846

Library of Congress Control Number: 2022943547

Notice: The information in this book is true and complete to the best of our knowledge. It is offered without guarantee on the part of the author or The History Press. The author and The History Press disclaim all liability in connection with the use of this book.

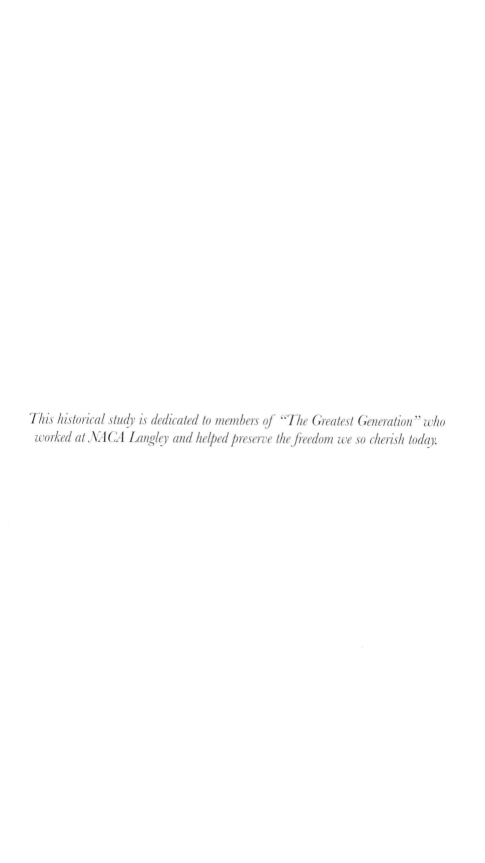

This historical study is dedicated to members of "The Greatest Generation" who worked at NACA Langley and helped preserve the freedom we so cherish today.

CONTENTS

Contents

ACKNOWLEDGEMENTS

The author would like to thank several important individuals who contributed to this fascinating history of how the NACA Langley Memorial Aeronautical Laboratory contributed to the Allied victory in World War II. I would like to thank my wife, Lesa, and sons, Patrick and Ryan, for their constant support and patience with me in preparation of this book.

Many thanks to my father, Joseph R. Chambers, who retired as a NASA Langley division chief in 1998 after thirty-six years of service to the agency and his country, for serving as a technical consultant in writing this book.

As always, special thanks go to Holly Reed and the staff of the U.S. National Archives at College Park, Maryland, Still Pictures Branch, for photographic support for this project.

Special thanks go to Mr. Keith Loftin, son of the late Mr. Laurence K. "Larry" Loftin Jr., former director for aeronautics at the NASA Langley Research Center, for providing his father's unpublished and unfinished manuscript, "A Research Pilot's World as Seen from the Cockpit of a NASA Engineer-Pilot," as well as his father's vast NACA/NASA Langley photo collection. Great thanks also go to the family of Donald L. Loving, for contributing Don's extensive NACA/NASA Langley photo collection for use in this project.

Special thanks also go to Kate Jenkins, acquisitions editor at The History Press, for securing publication of this work, her invaluable editorial assistance and her fantastic support for this project.

INTRODUCTION

When America entered World War II on December 8, 1941, it was ill prepared for battle. The nation's naval, army and marine corps air forces possessed air fleets that featured largely obsolescent aircraft that were inferior performance-wise and outnumbered by the Axis nations' military air fleets. By 1945, however, the United States' air forces were equipped with some of the world's most advanced combat aircraft and technologies, largely thanks to the war-winning aeronautical research efforts conducted by the National Advisory Committee for Aeronautics' (NACA's) Langley Memorial Aeronautical Laboratory (LMAL) in Hampton, Virginia. These remarkable research efforts, as described in this book, ultimately helped spur Allied victory in the war.

During the early years of the war, America's military air fleets were outclassed by enemy opposition in the air. For example, during the Battles of the Coral Sea and Midway, the U.S. Navy was still using obsolescent Douglas TBD Devastator torpedo bombers, which were often easily shot down by fast, nimble Japanese Mitsubishi A6M2 Zero fighters. When the venerable Devastator's replacement, the more advanced Grumman TBF Avenger, came online, the prototype aircraft was sent to the LMAL for extensive wind-tunnel and flight testing that helped make the aircraft one of the most advanced torpedo bombers of World War II. In addition, the U.S. Navy's premier fleet defender at the time, the Grumman F4F Wildcat, was inferior to the Japanese Zero in terms of performance. The U.S. Army's premier air-superiority fighter at the time, the Curtiss P-40 Tomahawk/

Warhawk, was inferior to German fighters such as the Messerschmitt Bf-109 and Focke-Wulf Fw-190. U.S. Army heavy bombers, such as the Consolidated B-24 Liberator and Boeing B-17 Flying Fortress, during the early years of the war, suffered heavy losses from enemy fighters and flak, and many invaluable bomber aircrews were lost when their aircraft were forced to make water landings (ditch) in the oceans due to extensive damage sustained in combat. These were some of the issues confronting U.S. war planners, aircraft industry leaders and the military services during the early years of World War II.

Formed in 1915 "to supervise and direct the scientific study of the problems of flight with a view to their practical solution," the NACA established itself over the next twenty-five years as one of the world's finest research organizations. When World War II began in 1939, the NACA employed a mere five hundred workers and maintained a budget slightly in excess of $4 million. To meet the demands of the war, a special partnership was quickly forged between NACA researchers, industry designers and military planners. The LMAL possessed world-class and unique aeronautical research facilities and flight research operations, making it ideally suited for enhancing America's military aviation arsenal and performing the monumental task of spurring Allied victory in World War II.

PART I

·················

AERONAUTICAL RESEARCH PERFORMED IN GROUND FACILITIES

When World War I began in 1914, the European nations each had over one thousand aircraft in their military air arsenals. In stark contrast, the United States had only twenty-three aircraft in its arsenal. To help industry jump-start aircraft development in the United States, Congress approved the formation of the National

Due to the increased threat of German aerial attack and the presence of German U-boats off the U.S. East Coast, the Army Air Forces decided to camouflage NACA Langley facilities by applying a coat of olive-drab paint in 1942. This photo, taken in 1943, depicts various camouflaged NACA facility buildings (*from left to right*): the Full-Scale Tunnel, 20-Foot Spin Tunnel, 12-Foot Free-Flight Tunnel, 15-Foot Free-Spinning Tunnel, 19-Foot Pressure Tunnel and Tow Tank.

Advisory Committee for Aeronautics (NACA), the predecessor government agency to today's National Aeronautics and Space Administration (NASA). In 1917, an area near Hampton, Virginia, was selected as the site for the agency's first research laboratory. Established as the nation's first civilian-led aeronautical research laboratory, the Langley Memorial Aeronautical Laboratory (LMAL) would go on to profoundly impact the field of aeronautics, not only in America but also around the world. During the years between World War I and World War II, numerous aeronautical research facilities were constructed at the LMAL that would serve as crucial tools in assisting the development of the aircraft needed to fight and win the war. These facilities proved to be significant contributors to providing design theories and data, problem-solving and evaluations of emerging aircraft concepts.

1

VARIABLE DENSITY TUNNEL (VDT)

In 1922, a radical, new, "game-changing" research that immensely affected the progress of aeronautics globally commenced in a new wind tunnel at the NACA LMAL. The wind tunnel, consisting of a steel pressure cylinder manufactured at the Newport News Shipyard in Virginia, was called the Variable Density Tunnel (VDT). The VDT was built to assist in the development and study of advanced low-drag airfoils at high Reynolds numbers. In the VDT, airfoils could be studied at a total of twenty atmospheres. In addition to consisting of a pressure shell, the VDT also possessed a drive motor and pressure line from a compressor.

A design team of researchers headed by Max M. Munk, who emigrated from Göttingen, Germany, to America and NACA Langley, designed the VDT. Munk was an ingenious student of the famous German professor Ludwig Prandtl. Munk and his American research assistants, Ira H. Abbott and Albert Von Doenhoff, worked to develop a detailed, comprehensive catalog or "bible" of low-drag airfoils that were ultimately incorporated on Allied aircraft designs before and during World War II (from the late 1930s to 1945).

Over one hundred airfoils were tested in the VDT. VDT researchers, including Eastman N. Jacobs, continued to work low-drag and boundary layer problems related to airfoils in their facility during the war. They soon received encouraging laboratory results that led to the advocacy for a new low-turbulence tunnel at the NACA LMAL. This advocacy later led to the development of the NACA Langley Low Turbulence Pressure Tunnel (LTPT).

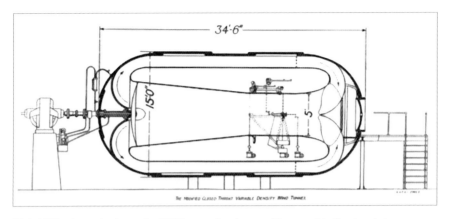

This 1928 schematic shows the VDT operational setup. The wood-built, closed-throat, annular-return VDT was enclosed in a pressurized tank and had a top speed of 51 miles per hour.

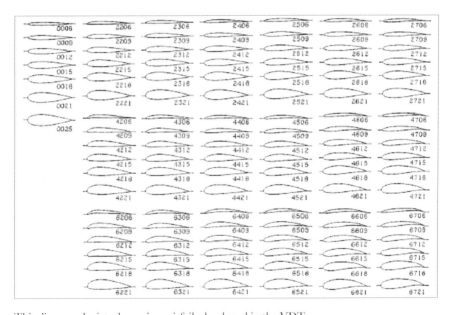

This diagram depicts the various airfoils developed in the VDT.

PROPELLER RESEARCH TUNNEL (PRT)

F ollowing World War I, the NACA sought to study propeller efficiency problems precipitated by the reduction of propeller performance at the tips at high speeds.[1] Navy engineer Fred Weick recommended in 1923 that the NACA undertake the construction of a wind tunnel possessing a twenty-foot-diameter throat and the capability to attain speeds approaching 100 miles per hour (mph) to conduct full-scale propeller tests. In 1925, construction efforts led by Director of Aeronautical Research George W. Lewis, commenced at NACA Langley on what would become known as the Propeller Research Tunnel (PRT). Construction of the new facility was finished by 1927. The facility became the first large-scale wind tunnel at the NACA LMAL. The PRT was also the third wind tunnel at the laboratory.

The PRT, the primary purpose of which was to study the aerodynamic efficiency of propellers on radial engine aircraft, commenced operations in 1927 and ultimately remained operational until 1950. The facility proved to be a critical research tool in drag-reduction efforts of early American aircraft. The PRT also proved to be a critical research tool in the derivation of the NACA Cowling, for which the NACA received its first Collier Trophy in 1929. The facility utilized two 1,000-horsepower (hp) diesel submarine engines and an eight-blade, twenty-seven-foot-diameter fan. The PRT also possessed the capability to generate a twenty-foot air stream at 110 miles per hour.[2]

During the war, the PRT was used to perform propeller airfoil research ranging up to high-speed propellers. The PRT was also used to study the

Side view of a gliding torpedo mounted in the test section of the PRT for wind-tunnel tests in 1942. The gliding torpedo was designed to be dropped from an aircraft at a high altitude.

A view from above of the gliding torpedo mounted in the test section of the PRT for wind-tunnel tests in 1942.

aerodynamic qualities of special aerial weapons, including an aerial torpedo that was to be dropped by a torpedo bomber and that would glide down to the surface of the water. In addition, the facility was used to study the aerodynamic efficiency of multi-blade propellers.

Research performed in the PRT revealed that engine location and the use of retractable landing gear significantly enhanced drag reduction. These revelations and further research performed in the PRT led to the utilization of data generated from these research efforts in the designs of a multitude of U.S. World War II aircraft. These aircraft included the Boeing B-17 Flying Fortress, the Consolidated B-24 Liberator, USAAF Douglas C-47 Skytrain and U.S. Navy R4D "Gooney Bird."

LOW TURBULENCE PRESSURE TUNNEL (LTPT)

D uring the late 1930s and the 1940s, airfoil research performed by engineers in the NACA Langley LTPT led to the development of new, revolutionary low-drag airfoils. Further work led to the development of the laminar flow airfoil by researcher Eastman N. Jacobs. The laminar flow airfoil was unique in that layers of air flowed completely smoothly over the wing's surface, resulting in greatly reduced drag. When an aircraft, the design of which utilized the laminar flow airfoil, was flying at cruising speed, the new airfoil produced predominantly laminar flow.

Through the utilization of low-drag wings, aircraft were then able to attain high speeds at cruise conditions and longer range. These advantages led the British to request that North American engineers incorporate the NACA laminar flow airfoil concept in the design of a new piston-engine air superiority fighter that would prove to be a "Game Changer" during the Second World War: the North American P-51 Mustang. A prototype of the aircraft, the XP-51A, was flight-tested at Langley and demonstrated extraordinary capabilities, leading both engineers and test pilots to become extremely excited about the aircraft. During World War II, the Mustang excelled as a long-range escort fighter for heavy strategic bombers while totally outclassing most Axis fighters in aerial combat.

Additional low-drag airfoil research performed in the LTPT led to the development of a second laminar flow airfoil series that was ultimately incorporated into the designs of the Bell P-63 Kingcobra, Douglas A-26 Invader and America's first jets, the Bell P-59 Airacomet and Lockheed P-80 Shooting Star.

Right: In the late 1930s and early 1940s, NACA Langley researcher Eastman N. Jacobs developed the laminar-flow airfoil through research performed in the NACA Langley LTPT. This revolutionary new airfoil ultimately helped make the North American P-51 Mustang a "game changer" in World War II.

Below: An aerial view of the LTPT at NACA Langley in April 1940.

O·8·852L·4IR (4·16·40·2:00P)(12·300) *Three Dimensional Wind Tunnel-NACA - L.F.,Va.*

Opposite, top: Construction of the LTPT in 1940.

Opposite, bottom: Langley's staff of airfoil experts used theoretical and experimental tools to further advance the families of laminar-flow airfoils developed by Eastman Jacobs during the war. The experimental work in the Two-Dimensional Low Turbulence Pressure Tunnel extended earlier research results to develop second-generation laminar-flow airfoil families of varying thickness ratios. Shown here in 1945 is a model display of airfoils produced at the facility.

Above: An airfoil model, mounted in the test section of the NACA Langley Two-Dimensional Low Turbulence Pressure Tunnel, is prepped for tests on March 18, 1939.

Left: An airfoil model, mounted in the test section of the NACA Langley LTPT, is prepped for tests in 1945.

Below: The curvature of the laminar-flow airfoil is displayed in this side view of a P-51D Mustang fighter. *Joseph Chambers.*

Interestingly, one of the NACA low-drag aerodynamic airfoils developed by Langley during the 1930s was the low-drag NACA 2213 series airfoil, ultimately incorporated in the wing designs of all variants (marks) of the British Supermarine Spitfire and Seafire.

FULL-SCALE TUNNEL (FST)

I n 1931, a unique wind tunnel became operational at NACA Langley that enabled engineers to study the aerodynamic qualities of actual full-size aircraft. This facility, the largest wind tunnel in the world at the time, featured a thirty-by-sixty-foot test section that was large enough to accommodate actual aircraft and large aircraft components, including actual operations of engines. The wind tunnel was named the Full-Scale Tunnel (FST). During World War II, perhaps no other NACA Langley aeronautical research facility had a more profound impact on the American war effort than the lab's FST. In this facility, important "drag cleanup" studies were performed on fighter, dive bomber and torpedo bomber aircraft as well as fuselage and inner-inner wing sections of some light bomber aircraft. This work led to design modifications that greatly enhanced the aerodynamic performance of these aircraft. Important engine cooling studies of aircraft engines were also performed in the FST. In addition, the NACA FST team performed cockpit environment studies whereby dangerous carbon monoxide levels in the cockpit produced from the operation of an aircraft's engine were significantly reduced. High-lift aircraft takeoff and landing studies aimed at reducing the size of an aircraft's wings were undertaken in the FST. This greatly enhanced the stowage capability of carrier-based aircraft, enabling more of the aircraft type to be embarked in aircraft carriers.

Drag Cleanup Studies

"Drag cleanup" was the most significant research performed by the NACA during World War II. Drag, the resistance to airflow, has been a major stumbling block for engineers and experimentalists since the infancy of heavier-than-air flight, and these innovators have struggled to minimize its inhibiting effects. Between 1938 and 1940, NACA Langley engineers conceived a method using its mammoth FST to measure drag and recommend to the aircraft manufacturer how to best solve the problems. The U.S. military reacted with great enthusiasm to the results obtained from this new process, which became known as "drag cleanup," because it provided a solution to technical problems and was quick and inexpensive. These factors caused the military to request that the NACA test almost every new prototype.

Throughout the war, drag cleanup studies were conducted at NACA Langley and the new NACA Ames laboratory, which had put into operation an even larger full-scale tunnel, in California. Drag cleanup studies began by placing an actual aircraft into one of the full-scale wind tunnels, removing all of the antennas and other items protruding from the aircraft fuselage and, finally, taping up the entire airplane surface. Measurements were then made of the "aerodynamically smooth" aircraft. The engineers would gradually remove the tape strips and determine the drag generated from every part of the aircraft. The final report of each study identified the problems and offered suggestions as to how to solve them. Drag cleanup recommendations were confirmed through extensive flight research conducted by the NACA.

Drag cleanup work often entailed the reshaping of an inlet or relocating it on the aircraft's fuselage, altering the shape of an aircraft's canopy, modifying an aircraft's cockpit ventilation system or relocating the antenna along the fuselage. These minor modifications produced mostly modest gains in drag reduction, but when combined, they produced significant increases in speed.

A prime example of how drag cleanup work significantly enhanced an aircraft's performance was the Bell P-39 Airacobra. When the aircraft rolled off the assembly line, it possessed a top speed of 340 mph. NACA Langley engineers performed two months of drag cleanup work on the aircraft, resulting in a new top speed of 392 mph. Through their important drag cleanup work, Langley engineers helped the Army avoid a financially costly and time-consuming total redesign of the airplane, which now met the Army's specifications.

Numerous other World War II fighter aircraft experienced significant performance enhancements as a result of Langley drag cleanup studies.

Before it served as an NACA Langley drag cleanup subject, the Curtiss P-40 possessed a top speed of 330 mph. Following the application of modifications recommended by Langley FST engineers as a result of drag cleanup work, the aircraft's top speed was increased to 360 mph. Resulting drag cleanup data obtained from work performed on the P-41 led to design enhancements that were later applied to the P-43 and Republic P-47 Thunderbolt. Drag cleanup work performed on the Chance Vought F4U Corsair led to minor modifications that raised the fleet defender's top speed by 15 mph. The NACA Langley work also showed that the top speed of the Corsair's counterpart, the Grumman F6F Hellcat, could be raised by 19 mph. These two primary U.S. Navy fleet defenders would go on to account for the majority of aerial victories scored by the Navy / Marine Corps in the Pacific Theater.

The significance of drag cleanup studies conducted in the NACA Langley FST was best demonstrated in the summer of 1942, when aeronautical engineer John P. "Jack" Reeder headed drag cleanup studies of the Grumman XTBF-1, the prototype of the Navy Avenger torpedo bomber. These studies proved to be the most extensive aerodynamic studies performed by the Full-Scale Tunnel research team to that date and remain as primary examples of drag reduction in new aeronautical technologies. Moreover, these studies are still applicable to piston-engine general aviation aircraft today. Reeder and his associate engineer, William J. Biebel, conducted a systematic study starting with drag measurements of the Avenger completely faired and sealed. This process progressed in consecutive stages until the aircraft was restored to its service state. Control-effectiveness measurements were recorded in power-on and off states, cooling-air pressure measurements recorded, canopy and turret air load pressure distribution measurements recorded and wing-mounted radar installation effects evaluated.[3] The final NACA report to the Navy's Bureau of Aeronautics provided the U.S. military with a "bible" of data for the evaluation of the effects of airplane components and physical state on drag.

Opposite, top: In 1939, the first XP-39 was tested in the Langley Full-Scale Tunnel. The XP-39 and its later variants were the subjects of extensive drag cleanup studies in the FST. The Airacobra ultimately benefited significantly in terms of performance enhancement from these studies and went on to become a mainstay of the USAAF in both the European and Pacific Theaters of World War II.

Opposite, bottom: The XP-40 Tomahawk prototype aircraft was also the subject of extensive drag cleanup studies in the Langley FST in 1939. The main objective of these studies was to improve the top speed of the aircraft via drag reduction, which the studies succeeded in achieving. As a result, the Tomahawk went on to serve as a premier fighter for the USAAF during the early years of World War II.

A U.S. Navy Vought F4U-1 Corsair undergoes drag cleanup testing in the Langley FST in November 1942. Note that the propeller, aerials and protuberances have been removed and tape applied to all cracks, crevices and control surface hinges. Through this research process, engineers were able to determine the minimum possible drag. Drag produced by specific components was measured by conducting tests with the tape removed. The Corsair ultimately benefited from the Langley drag cleanup studies and went on to help the U.S. Navy achieve air superiority against the Japanese in the Pacific.

A Lockheed YP-38 Lightning prototype undergoes compressibility effects testing in the FST on Christmas Eve 1941.

The U.S. Navy Vought F4U-1 Corsair being tested in the FST with power on after undergoing drag-reduction modifications on December 24, 1942.

A Grumman F6F-3 Hellcat undergoes drag cleanup testing in the FST on March 22, 1943. Like the Corsair, the Hellcat benefited greatly from the Langley drag cleanup studies and went on to register more than half of all U.S. Navy aerial victories in the Pacific.

Top: A view through the entrance cone of the FST of a North American P-51B Mustang mounted in the test section of the tunnel for drag cleanup tests on September 22, 1943.

Middle: A side view of a North American P-51B Mustang mounted in the test section of the tunnel for drag cleanup tests on September 22, 1943.

Bottom: A view through the entrance cone of the FST of America's first jet fighter, the Bell YP-59A Airacomet, mounted in the test section of the tunnel for drag cleanup tests in 1944. The Airacomet was vastly inferior in terms of performance capability to the German Messerschmitt Me-262 Schwalbe, or "Swallow," the world's first combat operational jet fighter.

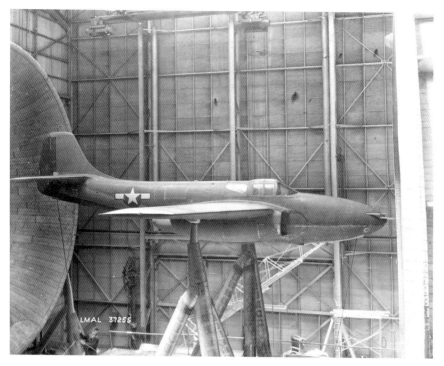

The Bell YP-59A Airacomet was tested in the Langley Full-Scale Tunnel in 1944 to determine means of improving the performance, stability and control of the airplane. The Langley staff had not been briefed on the Army's secret project to develop the P-59 until mid-1943. Although the airplane used laminar-flow airfoils, its high-speed performance was very disappointing when compared with competitive German aircraft such as the Messerschmitt Me-262. The P-59 had a thrust-to-weight ratio that was 30 percent greater than that of the Me-262, but its top speed was 130 miles per hour slower than the German jet. The P-59 did not use wing high-lift devices for landing, instead relying on increased wing area to reduce landing speed. In contrast, the Me-262 used lift devices and a much smaller wing, resulting in less drag at cruise conditions. Modifications suggested by the Langley test would have increased the top speed of the Airacomet by about 27 miles per hour. During one of the first power-on tests in the tunnel, the left engine-bay area of the airplane caught fire and burned extensively, damaging the cockpit area in the process. Apparently, the decision of whether to fuel the jet engines from the airplane's onboard fuel tanks or from an external fuel source was late coming, and in the process a tunnel technician had begun to reroute incoming fuel lines when the decision to fuel from onboard tanks was made, resulting in an undetected fuel leak. The technician was known thereafter as "Hacksaw" Smith. Many other Langley organizations contributed to the development of the P-59, especially the 8-Foot High Speed Tunnel.

Top: Side view of the Grumman XTBF-1 Avenger prototype undergoing drag cleanup testing in the FST in June 1942.

Bottom: Frontal view of a Curtiss SB2C-4 Helldiver mounted in the FST for drag cleanup testing in 1945.

ENGINE COOLING STUDIES

Throughout World War II, the military often discovered that some of its aircraft, operating in the harsh desert heat of North Africa and tropical heat of the South Pacific, experienced engine overheating problems. The military requested the assistance of NACA Langley engineers to find solutions to the problems. Consequently, NACA Langley engineers often made recommendations to industry on how their production aircraft could be modified to correct these engine cooling problems. During the war, NACA Langley formed a Cooling College to inform industry teams on the latest NACA methods and solutions to problems.

In January 1941, the Army requested that then NACA Langley FST aeronautical engineer Jack Reeder (he transferred to the NACA Langley Flight Research Division as an engineering test pilot in 1942) and Herbert A. "Hack" Wilson lead wind-tunnel studies to improve the engine cooling and aerodynamic performance characteristics of the Douglas A-20A Havoc, a new twin-engine attack bomber. Army and Douglas flight tests indicated that while engine cooling was satisfactory in cruise flight, temperatures of the cylinder head rose to levels that were in excess of the limits permitted for high-power climb conditions. An attempt was made by Douglas to solve the cooling issue by cutting eight holes in the cowling behind the cylinder baffles. However, this resulted in additional drag being produced, reducing the top speed of the aircraft. New engine cowling installations were developed by Reeder and Wilson following their extensive study of the Havoc's cooling problem. These new engine cowling installations could be applied to later A-20 variants. The NACA study results produced numerous satisfactory cowling arrangement possibilities. These possibilities included the use of blowers and ejector stacks. NACA Langley's suggested modifications were ultimately incorporated in the designs of later A-20 versions. The A-20 would go on to become quite effective in the ground attack / low-altitude bomber role during World War II.

Langley researchers at the Full-Scale Tunnel and the Propeller Research Tunnel were widely sought for consultation by industry and the military services for their expertise in the areas of engine cooling and cowling technology in the early 1940s. In coordination with the Army's liaison officer, Colonel Carl Greene, a new Langley office informally referred to as the "Cooling and Cowling College" was established. It provided the industry and military with the latest technology and lessons learned by the NACA, particularly for radial air-cooled engines. Clinton Dearborn, former head of the Full-Scale Tunnel, led the office, which was located on the third floor of the East Shop building. This photograph of leaders in engine installation technology was taken during a visit by Dr. George Lewis of NACA headquarters in November 1940. Those present were (*left to right*): Dr. George Lewis of NACA; Clinton Dearborn, head of the Langley group; Colonel Greene; Peter Torraco of Republic Aviation Company; William Richards of Wright Aeronautical; H.S. Ditsch of the Curtiss Company; Dr. H.J.E. Reid of Langley; and James Thomson of Pratt & Whitney.

This Douglas A-20A twin engine light attack bomber had its outer wing panels removed and is mounted in the FST for engine cooling/aerodynamic performance-improvement testing.

Engine cooling studies were performed on this Consolidated B-24 engine assembly setup on the beach outside of the FST near the Back River on November 3, 1942.

This page: These two photos depict a B-24D engine assembly in its original state with 10-degree flap deflection.

A B-24D engine assembly with original nacelle mounted for engine cooling tests in the FST.

A view of a modified B-24D engine nacelle. The nacelle was modified as a result of NACA Langley engine cooling research.

An XB-39 engine assembly mounted in the FST for engine cooling studies on November 4, 1943.

HIGH-LIFT TAKEOFF AND LANDING STUDIES

FST researchers performed important high-lift takeoff and landing research to reduce the size of the wings on U.S. naval carrier-borne aircraft during World War II. Through this important research, aircraft such as the Chance Vought F4U Corsair had their wing sizes reduced without adversely affecting their carrier landing capabilities so that with their wings in the folded position they could be easily accommodated on aircraft elevators aboard carriers and more of their type could be accommodated on the carriers. More important, smaller wings on the aircraft provided less cruise drag and weight.

ARMY YR-4B HOVERFLY HELICOPTER STUDIES

In October 1944, NACA Langley conducted wind-tunnel studies of the world's first practical helicopter, the Army YR-4B Hoverfly, in the FST. These studies were aimed at determining the aerodynamic behavior and rotor characteristics of the rotorcraft. Results of these studies were later verified through flight tests of the Navy version of the Hoverfly, the HNS-1, conducted at NACA Langley in March 1945.

A Vought F4U Corsair is positioned on a simulated carrier flight deck in the FST for high-lift takeoff and landing research studies.

The Army YR-4B undergoing aerodynamic evaluation in the FST in October 1944.

COCKPIT ENVIRONMENT STUDIES

NACA Langley performed important cockpit environment studies in the FST that significantly reduced dangerous carbon monoxide levels in the cockpits of World War II aircraft. Perhaps the most impressive work was performed on the Brewster F2F Buffalo.

GENERAL MOTORS AERIAL TORPEDO STUDIES

An interesting series of FST studies were conducted at NACA Langley in August 1941, at the request of the Army, on the General Motors Aerial Torpedo. This aircraft was an unmanned flying bomb designated the GM A-1. Unmanned aviation pioneer Charles F. Kettering of General Motors proposed a radio-controlled flying bomb to the Army Air Corps in September 1939. Kettering previously achieved fame by inventing an unmanned flying bomb in 1918 that became known as the Kettering "Bug." World War I was still raging at the time, and the Army placed an order for fifty Bugs. But the war ended before it could be used in combat. Following launch from a track, the flying bomb was supposed to fly a straight route to the enemy. The propeller revolution number was tracked by a counter, and when the flying bomb reached its target, the engine fuel supply was to be cut off, at which time a cam locked into position to fold the wings. The Bug would then fall to its ground target and explode. No direct control was provided for the Bug, and its climb was controlled through the use of an altitude sensor and pneumatic controls.

Power was supplied to the GM A-1 through the use of a 200-hp piston engine. The flying bomb was to be launched from a four-wheeled dolly. It was capable of carrying a 500-pound bomb and had a range of four hundred miles. The pilotless drone possessed elevator and rudder controls that were automatically operated by an altimeter and a directional gyro. Following a 100-mph catapult launch, the aircraft would climb to a preset altitude and fly at a speed of 200 mph along a preset course. The aircraft spanned 21 feet and had a weight of approximately 1,250 pounds when fully loaded. The Army ordered ten prototypes in 1941. A request for a wind-tunnel evaluation in the Full-Scale Tunnel was also made.

Reeder and G. Merritt Preston conducted extensive studies aimed at determining the control positions for proper trim of the aircraft. Powered

The General Motors Aerial Torpedo or GM A-1 mounted in the FST for aerodynamic performance, stability and control characteristics testing in August 1941.

tests were also performed to determine the effects of propeller slipstream. Stability was evaluated about all three axes, and a prediction of flying characteristics was made. According to the report to the Army, "The static stability and control effectiveness of the airplane were found to be ample and that the top speed of the drone would be about 198 miles per hour based on the tunnel data."[4] The wind-tunnel test results revealed that there were no issues encountered that would hinder the success of the design. However, several crashes, caused by problems with the launch and guidance systems, brought about a cancellation of the program in 1943.

VOUGHT-SIKORSKY V-173 "FLYING PANCAKE" STUDIES

One of the strangest aircraft subjects tested in the NACA Langley FST was the Vought-Sikorsky V-173 "Flying Pancake." FST tests were performed on this unusual aircraft beginning in November 1941. This aerial oddity was designed by Charles H. Zimmerman, one of the LMAL's most innovative aeronautical engineers. Zimmerman excelled in applied aerodynamics and flight dynamics research. He was the designer and development leader of the NACA Langley Spin Tunnel and Free-Flight Tunnel. He also invented the Hiller "Flying Platform," tested by the Army in the 1950s. During the 1930s, Zimmerman sought to develop the "Pancake" shape as a concept capable of providing Short Take-Off and Landing (STOL) capability. The low-aspect-ratio, almost circular wing and large counter-rotating propellers of the Flying Pancake design afforded it the potential for extremely low approach and landing speeds. Through small-scale model studies conducted from 1933 to 1937 at NACA Langley, Zimmerman managed to mature his unconventional concept. After gaining the approval of the NACA, Zimmerman proposed his unique design to the United Aircraft Corporation in 1937 and was brought aboard United's Chance Vought Aircraft Division to serve as a project engineer that same year. His unusual design became known as the V-173, which was designated as a flight-worthy experimental flight demonstrator for the pancake-wing concept. From this experimental testbed, further advanced military versions were to be developed.

The Navy's Bureau of Aeronautics requested that the V-173 undergo extensive testing in the Full-Scale Tunnel to evaluate the aerodynamic performance, drag characteristics and airflow phenomena associated with the design (most notably, propeller slipstream effects). While it was planned to power the lightweight design with two 75-hp engines at the time of the wind-tunnel tests, provisions were being made to power high-speed military versions of the aircraft with two 2,000-hp engines. The NACA hoped that the wind-tunnel tests would yield data deemed "useful" in the development of the higher-powered aircraft, which ultimately became the XF5U-1.

Jack Reeder was heavily involved in the tests, from collecting conventional data utilizing the tunnel scale system to making his own measurements of the aircraft's control characteristics. Jack once said, "I sat in the cockpit while the plane was mounted in the wind tunnel measuring forces using hand-held springs."[5] He also measured pressure distributions for power-on and power-off conditions.

Reeder and Gerald W. "Jerry" Brewer performed extensive testing and provided a detailed description of the V-173's aerodynamic characteristics. They made several revealing conclusions concerning the aerodynamic effects of the aircraft's large propellers in their memorandum report to the Navy: "(1) the inherently high induced drag of a low-aspect-ratio circular wing can be partially compressed by the favorable interaction of large-diameter propellers operating ahead of the wing; (2) the effects of the operation of

Charles Zimmerman, the brilliant Langley researcher who designed the Langley 15-Foot Free-Spinning Tunnel and the Langley 12-Foot Free-Flight Tunnel, became interested in the use of unconventional pancake-shaped wings for providing extremely short takeoff-and-landing performance for increased safety of privately owned airplanes in 1933. His interest developed into free-flight model tests that verified the concept. Zimmerman left Langley in 1937 to join the Chance Vought Corporation, where he pursued the development of a radical demonstrator airplane known as the V-173 and Navy contracts for the concept. Affectionately known as the "Flying Pancake" and "Zimmer Skimmer," the wood-and-fabric testbed completed many successful flight tests, including an evaluation by Charles Lindbergh and several Navy pilots. This photograph shows the V-173 mounted in the FST for aerodynamic testing. In 1941, Chance Vought was awarded a follow-on Navy contract for an advanced fighter version based on the V-173 concept known as the XF5U-1. In addition to its predicted short-field capability, the new fighter would be faster than other naval aircraft, with a top speed over 40 mph faster than the fastest naval fighter at the time, the Vought F4U Corsair. The Navy hoped to utilize the short-takeoff-and-landing and high-speed characteristics of the XF5U-1 on small aircraft carriers to protect the naval fleets in the Pacific from Kamikaze suicide attacks by Japanese aircraft. Unfortunately, development problems arose involving the propellers of the advanced design, resulting in significant delays in the project until beyond the end of the war, and the Navy canceled the project. *NASA Langley Research Center via Larry Loftin.*

large-diameter propellers ahead of a wing are equivalent to an increase in the wing span since it results in increasing the mass of air to which downward momentum is imparted by the lifting force; (3) the reduction in the induced drag and increased propulsive efficiency obtained with propeller operation is dependent only in a minor way on the relative direction of the rotation of the propeller and the tip vortices; (4) propeller operation on the V-173 airplane arrangement effects a large decrease in the longitudinal stability due to the lift on the propellers and the slipstream rotation at the tail; and (5) rotation of the propellers opposite to the present arrangement so that they turn in the same direction as the tip vortices would result in greatly increased stability with only slight decreases in the propulsive efficiency."[6]

The V-173 STOL flight demonstrator flew for the first time on November 23, 1942. The aircraft performed well in flight. Back in 1941, the Navy had awarded Chance Vought a contract to further develop the Flying Pancake design, under the designation XF5U-1. In mid-1945, large-scale model tests of the XF5U-1 were performed in the Full-Scale Tunnel at the request of the Navy. The Navy gave serious consideration to using the XF5U-1, with its excellent short-takeoff-and-landing and high-speed characteristics, as an interceptor to counter Japanese Kamikaze aircraft that posed a grave threat to U.S. naval warships in the Pacific during the closing months of

The Vought-Sikorsky V-173 performing a test flight. *Larry Loftin.*

A powered model of the Chance Vought XF5U-1 mounted in the FST for tests to evaluate the aerodynamic characteristics of the unique aircraft design in 1945.

The XF5U-1 never flew but proved to be one of World War II's most unconventional aircraft designs. *Smithsonian Institution via NASA Langley Research Center.*

World War II. However, the war ended before the aircraft could be used in combat, and the service entry of the jet fighter caused the Navy to abandon the XF5U-1 program. Although the program was terminated and the aircraft was never flown, it did contribute invaluable design data for postwar V/STOL aircraft designs.

REPUBLIC XP-69 STUDIES

In the early 1940s, the Republic Aviation Company pursued the development of an unconventional fighter design, requested by the Army, that became known as the XP-69. The aircraft was to be powered by a Wright R-2160 liquid-cooled radial engine. The engine was placed behind the cockpit, with the aircraft being propelled by contra-rotating three-blade propellers. The aircraft was intended for high-altitude missions and featured a pressurized cockpit. The aircraft also featured two 37-millimeter cannon and four 0.50-caliber machine guns for armament.

Langley Full-Scale Tunnel tests of a powered 0.75-scale model of the XP-69 were requested by the Army Air Corps Materiel Command to evaluate the longitudinal and lateral-directional stability and control behavior of the airplane configured with dual-rotating propellers. The huge XP-69 model utilized sheet-aluminum metal outer skins. Two ten-foot-diameter propellers, driven by two 25-horsepower electric motors positioned in the fuselage, were applied to the aircraft model. In years before the XP-69 model tests, the dual-rotating aircraft propeller concept was evaluated in the Langley Propeller Research Tunnel. The aircraft concept utilized slotted Fowler-type flaps as high-lift devices. Forces and moments on the model were evaluated for various angles of attack and sideslip. Evaluations were conducted in both the propellers-off and propellers-running modes. Evaluations were made with the flaps in both the retracted and deflected positions. Evaluations were also made of propeller slipstream effects.

In August 1942, the Langley FST results showed that the aircraft was longitudinally stable through the full range of lift, but a substantial reduction in stability was experienced in the power-on state due to the direct contribution of the propeller's normal forces ahead of the center of gravity. Elevator Control was adequate under all test conditions. Identification was made of the possibility of dynamic lateral instability or "Dutch Roll" due to excessive dihedral effect and low directional stability under flaps-down

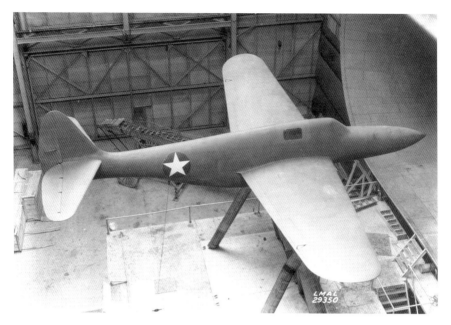

A Republic XP-69 model mounted in the FST for longitudinal and lateral stability and control characteristics testing. The aircraft featured contra-rotating propellers.

landing conditions when idling power. In comparison to other fighter aircraft of the time, the XP-69's roll control was low, while lateral stick forces at high speeds were found unsatisfactory. No asymmetry was found in yawing or rolling moments in the cruise or low angle of attack modes. It was also found that no aileron or rudder input was necessary for maintaining unyawed attitude in the normal operational state.

Although the XP-69 FST aerodynamic test results were encouraging, multiple setbacks were experienced in the development of the XP-69's engine. Consequently, the Army Air Corps ultimately abandoned the XP-69 project, choosing to further develop the Republic XP-72 instead. In May 1943, the XP-69 project was officially canceled, with only a single airplane having been produced.

CURTISS XP-55 ASCENDER STUDIES

Another unusual aircraft test subject that was studied in the NACA Langley FST during World War II was the Curtiss XP-55 Ascender. The Army

Air Corps sought the development of a radical fighter aircraft design in late 1939 and issued a request for proposals of such an aircraft. Curtiss-Wright Corporation answered the Army's request, proposing an unusual, free-floating canard, pusher-propeller design that utilized a swept-back wing. The airplane was called the XP-55 Ascender and also incorporated tricycle landing gear.

Curtiss-Wright was awarded the Army contract in June 1940, and development work on the XP-55 commenced soon thereafter. The Army contract requested first for the development of a powered wind-tunnel model for preliminary evaluation of the design. According to the contract, Curtiss-Wright was to furnish a wind-tunnel model, preliminary wind-tunnel data and provisions for a test aircraft. Curtiss-Wright managed to garner only a "lukewarm reception" from the Army following the construction and evaluation of a large aircraft concept model. Consequently, the company used its own funding to continue the development of its unique aircraft design. This further development resulted in the production of a full-scale flight demonstrator designated the CW-24B. The CW-24B was a fabric-covered, wooden-winged design and was to serve as a lightweight, low-powered flight demonstrator for the actual full-scale fighter aircraft.

A 0.25-scale model of the CW-24B was tested in a wind tunnel at the Massachusetts Institute of Technology and the NACA Langley 19-foot Pressure Tunnel in 1941. Flow separation on the outer swept-wing panels at high angles of attack was determined to be an issue of key concern during the early stages of both wind-tunnel test programs. This problem produced longitudinal instability ("pitch up") near stall. At the request of the Materiel Command of the Army Air Forces, the NACA conducted Langley Free-Flight Tunnel tests of a free-flying CW-24B model to study its flight characteristics in mid-1941. A 0.10-scale flying model was built for testing by late November. The first test subject was unpowered, after which another powered subject was slated for testing in 1942.

The Free-Flight Tunnel tests led to the discovery of numerous problems. The CW-24 was a tailless design that utilized vertical tail fins for directional stability. The test results indicated that the design was directionally unstable. The airplane possessed excessive geometric dihedral, and the ailerons possessed inadequate power. Longitudinal instability determined in other wind-tunnel tests was also encountered with this model. Concern was also raised regarding the longitudinal control system used for the free-floating canard. Upon allowance of the canard to float freely and align itself with the local flow at the nose, the longitudinal stability below stall was adequate, but when the pilot controlling the model held the elevator in the same position for just a few seconds, the model became dangerously longitudinally unstable. At NACA Langley, engineers suggested the installation of vertical fins at the wingtips, a reduction of the geometric wing dihedral angle, an increase of the aileron area by 25 percent and a review of the longitudinal control-system design. (The system design could have potentially caused stability problems for the fixed-canard state in critical flight regimes.) When the model was tested again in the Free-Flight Tunnel, the suggestions made by the NACA had already been incorporated. Changes were also made to the full-scale airplane, including the incorporation of engine cowl fins and modified wingtips. The second series of wind-tunnel tests proved to be successful, as the directional-stability issue had been corrected as a result of the incorporation of vertical fins at the wingtips. However, the excessive dihedral, inadequate aileron control and stick-fixed longitudinal instability issues persisted.

In December 1941, the CW-24B was test-flown for the first time at Muroc Bombing Range (now Edwards Air Force Base), California. Initial wind-tunnel tests showed that after experiencing longitudinal instability at stall, the aircraft would experience a "deep stall," in which it would trim at extremely high positive or negative angles of attack and descend in near-vertical flight, falling into an uncontrollable state at a nearly horizontal attitude. However, the CW-24B was incapable of spin recovery, and therefore, intentional spins were not tried in the preliminary flight-test program. The CW-24B made a total of 190 successful test flights. As a result, Curtiss-Wright was awarded an Army Air Corps contract for three flight-worthy XP-55 airplanes in July 1942.

Following the conclusion of the CW-24B flight-test program in May 1942, the Army Materiel Command obtained the flight demonstrator from Curtiss. The Army requested that Langley conduct an aerodynamic study of the aircraft in the FST. The NACA approved this study and commenced the FST study in October 1942. Langley engineers and staff adjusted the CW-24B's design to be more representative of the actual XP-55 design.

The full-scale test results matched up well with previous subscale model tests. On having the stick in the fixed position with the propeller removed, Langley engineers determined that the CW-24B was longitudinally unstable. It was found that with the stick free and the canard free-floating and the landing flaps retracted, longitudinal stability was maintainable at angles of attack below 12 degrees. However, the airplane displayed pitch-up at higher angles of attack. Langley engineers also discovered that a

The CW-24B or Curtiss XP-55 concept demonstrator mounted in the FST for longitudinal stability and control tests on October 27, 1942.

flap deflection of 45 degrees caused a reduction of the instability level once the stick was in a fixed position and improved stability in the free-stick position. Langley FST flow visualization test results indicated that the aircraft possessed a pitch-up tendency.

Ultimately, the XP-55 proved to be a "poor performer" when matched up with other contemporary conventional fighters of World War II. In addition, jet fighters began to emerge in the service inventories of several nations. As a result, the Army canceled the XP-55 program.

SPIN TUNNEL

During World War II, researchers at NACA Langley performed invaluable research regarding aircraft spinning. At the request of the Army and Navy, in excess of three hundred scale models of every aircraft in the U.S. inventory (including those proposed and/or actual in-service) were tested in the NACA Langley Spin Tunnel, the only operational spin tunnel in America during the war. This research provided information to test pilots and companies prior to the maiden flights of prototype aircraft. NACA Langley Spin Tunnel researchers performed additional testing for modifications to aircraft designs. The Langley Spin Tunnel research team also recommended spin recovery techniques to operational service pilots. In addition, the research team made recommendations for parachute size and configuration for obtaining satisfactory emergency spin recovery during first flight tests of aircraft.

Successful operation of a vertical free-spinning tunnel requires that the weight of the spinning model be supported by its upward-acting aerodynamic drag. During the years immediately preceding World War II, the size and weight of high-performance military aircraft rapidly increased from those of earlier biplanes. Langley researchers correctly anticipated that the 40-mph vertical airspeed capability of the existing 15-Foot Free-Spinning Tunnel would be insufficient for spinning tests of emerging U.S. aircraft. In 1941, a new 20-Foot Spin Tunnel designed by Oscar Seidman became operational with a maximum airspeed of 66 mph, providing a test capability for virtually all prototype and production aircraft during the war. This photograph, taken in 1941, shows a typical spinning test in the facility.

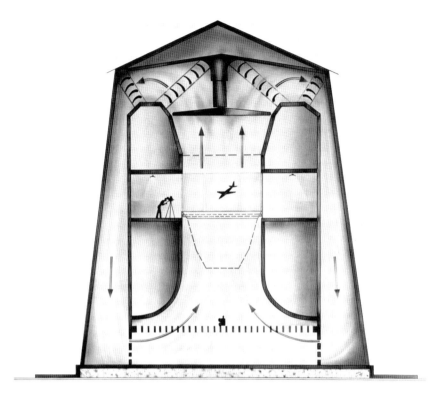

This sketch shows a cross-section of the flow circuit within the tunnel. The model was hand-launched with pre-rotation into the vertical airstream, and the tunnel operator adjusted the airspeed to maintain the model in front of the observers. Spinning motions were recorded on film, and the model's control surfaces are remotely moved to specified positions during attempts at spin recovery. At the end of the test, the speed was reduced, and the model settled into a net at the bottom of the test section, where it was grasped and retrieved with long tongs. With modifications and ongoing advances in data instrumentation and acquisition, the tunnel continues to operate today, having served the nation for over seventy-five years.

This Republic P-47 Thunderbolt model is being evaluated for spinning characteristics in the NACA Langley 20-Foot Vertical Spin Tunnel in 1942.

6

12-FOOT FREE-FLIGHT TUNNEL

In 1939, the 12-Foot Free-Flight Tunnel became operational at NACA Langley. This unique wind tunnel was designed to study the stability and control of aircraft designs in model form. This wind tunnel was used to evaluate the stability and control characteristics of numerous aircraft designs that saw combat in World War II. Models of the BT-9, XF2A-1, SBN-1, XF4U-1, Northrop N-1, a Glide Bomb, XP-56, Curtiss-Wright 24, XP-63, B-25, B-29, B-30, B-32, GB-5 Glide Bomb, GB-7, Navy Design No. BADR Gargoyle missile and XFG-1 glider were tested in the tunnel.

This North American XB-28 twin-engine bomber model was evaluated in the NACA Langley 12-Foot Free-Flight Tunnel on March 13, 1942.

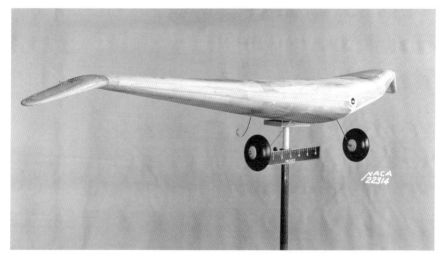

This Northrop N-1-M Flying Wing model was evaluated in the 12-Foot Free-Flight Tunnel on November 5, 1940.

An SBN-1 model in flight in the 12-Foot Free-Flight Tunnel on September 4, 1940.

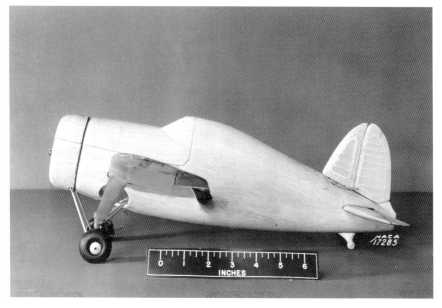

This Brewster XF2A-1 Buffalo model was evaluated in the 12-Foot Free-Flight Tunnel on April 4, 1939.

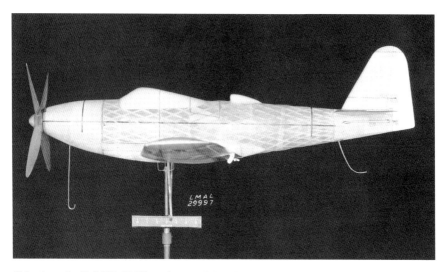

Side view of a Bell XP-63 Kingcobra model evaluated in the 12-Foot Free-Flight Tunnel on October 16, 1942.

7

16-FOOT HIGH-SPEED TUNNEL (HST)

In 1941, a new research facility opened at NACA Langley that offered a solution to cooling problems being experienced with air-cooled aircraft engines. The facility offered a quick and cheap solution through the testing of mounted full-scale engines and nacelles at various power settings. This tunnel testing also permitted temperature sensor data collection that could not be observed in free-flight.

Researchers at NACA Langley performed a variety of research in the 16-Foot HST during World War II. In addition to testing full-scale engine propulsion units, the facility also became the first research facility to conduct research aimed at finding solutions to high-speed aerodynamic problems with fighter aircraft at the time. These problems arose from inadequate efficiency experienced at high speeds. Research performed in the NACA Langley 16-Foot HST led to buffeting and flutter problem elimination.

In addition to providing military support in its wind tunnels, flight and laboratories, Langley conceived, constructed and operated engine and propeller outdoor test facilities for evaluations and solutions to propulsion issues that arose within the Army and Navy operational units. Shown are a B-24 Liberator bomber engine mounted on an engine test stand and an XSC-1 scout airplane engine stand with an instrumentation house in the picture. The B-24 project was conducted in response to an urgent request of the Army in early 1942 to analyze and solve engine overheating problems that were experienced by Army B-24 units operating out of North Africa. With heavy bomb loads and excessive heat in the desert, several units had to return to base because of engine overheating and failures. In a rapid-response mode, the staff of the Full-Scale Tunnel and Langley's shops and instrumentation organizations constructed a test apparatus, fabricated a B-24 propeller/nacelle/stub wing test article, as well as the additional equipment required for the task, including fuel lines, engine controls and instrumentation. The project was completed in the remarkable time of two weeks, and cooling-baffle modifications were quickly sent to North Africa and used with success. The XSC-1 test (shown here) was conducted for the Navy by the staff of the 16-Foot High-Speed Tunnel at a test stand to ensure adequate cooling for the Navy XSC-1 Seahawk in 1943. The dedication and responsiveness of Langley's staff to "911" calls from the military were major contributions to victory during World War II.

8

8-FOOT HIGH-SPEED TUNNEL (HST)

Another NACA Langley research facility that proved to be invaluable to the American war effort was the 8-Foot HST, constructed in 1936. In this facility, research was performed that led to a solution to the Lockheed P-38 Lightning tail separation problem experienced in flight testing of the aircraft. This problem arose from a new phenomenon being experienced by U.S. fighter pilots engaged in aerial combat with enemy aircraft.

During aerial combat in World War II, U.S. fighter pilots began experiencing a frightening, unexplained loss of control that developed when airflow over their aircraft surpassed the speed of sound, even though the aircraft was not flying faster than the speed of sound at the time. With no warning, the aircraft would suddenly plunge into an uncontrollable, steep dive. The phenomenon came as a surprise to industry and NACA engineers.

The NACA immediately conducted studies of this new phenomenon in the Langley 8-Foot HST. Long before World War II, researchers discovered that air is really a compressible fluid and, as aircraft approached the speed of sound, became extremely dense with great pressure, resulting in the formation of shock waves that altered the airflow over the wing surfaces. The initial test subject happened to be the Lockheed P-38 Lightning. The results of these wind-tunnel tests were confirmed through flight testing of the YP-38 (prototype of the Lightning series) by NACA Langley's Flight Research Division. The NACA's recommendations, however, were not adhered to by Lockheed due to the fact that the company sought a swift and cheap solution. Consequently, the NACA initiated a second set of research studies at its NACA

This page: High-speed testing of a Lockheed P-38 Lightning model began in the 8-Foot High-Speed Tunnel in February 1942. As had been expected by Kelly Johnson, at about 450 miles per hour, shock waves began to form on the upper surface of the inner-wing area. Disturbed airflow behind the shock waves violently impinged on the tail surfaces and caused loss of wing lift, resulting in the tail buffeting and diving tendencies that had been experienced in the fatal flight-test accident. Among the modifications evaluated during the investigation were a raised-tail configuration shown in the accompanying pictures taken on February 6, 1942. This modification was also found to be unacceptable; but after four months of testing, an extendable "dive-recovery flap" installed on the lower surface of the wing was found to be effective in providing lift when the compressibility problem was encountered, thereby enabling a pilot to pull the plane out of steep dives. The P-38 dive-recovery program was then moved from Langley to the West Coast, where Lockheed and the NACA Ames Aeronautical Laboratory further refined the concept. The dive-recovery flap concept was also applied to the P-47 Thunderbolt, the A-26 Invader, the P-59 Airacomet and the P-80 Shooting Star jet fighter.

This page: Demands on high-priority military testing in the 8-Foot High-Speed Tunnel at the time of the P-38 study included the development of the famous Boeing B-29 Superfortress bomber. Regarded as the most streamlined heavy bomber during World War II, the B-29 was a critical contributor to victory in the Pacific. This model, photographed in the tunnel on March 12, 1942, was tested by legendary Langley researchers John V. Becker and Donald D. Baals. Their analysis was completed in a very timely manner, resulting in a complimentary letter of praise in April to Langley from Boeing's Eddie Allen, Langley's first test pilot, who had risen to the position of director of flight and aerodynamics at the Boeing Aircraft Company. His letter stated, "The rapid development of the test and early availability of data greatly enhanced the value of the test and reduced the time required for conduct and analysis, appreciably assisting in a material speed-up of operations."

Langley actively recruited female workers to meet the increasing demand of the war effort and to offset the alarming loss of manpower as men were drafted and volunteered for military service or were transferred to the new NACA laboratories at Ames and AERL. These women were working in the Langley 8-Foot HST in 1943.

Ames Aeronautical Research Laboratory. This work built on the initial studies performed by NACA Langley. Ames engineers conceived three potential solutions. Ames researchers performed wind-tunnel studies supplemented by more important flight research studies aimed at simulating the conditions experienced during aerial combat. Despite giving no credit to the NACA, Lockheed sought a "quick fix" and decided to adopt an NACA dive flaps recommendation, which called for the addition of flaps on the wing lower surface. The addition of dive-recovery flaps ultimately resulted in enhanced pilot control of compressibility effects and of the aircraft when diving.

NACA dive-recovery flaps were ultimately incorporated in the designs of the P-47 Thunderbolt, A-26 Invader and America's first two jet fighters, the Bell P-59 Airacomet and Lockheed P-80 Shooting Star. In addition to attempting to find solutions to the compressibility problem, research performed in the tunnel led to an improvement in the performance of the Boeing B-29 Superfortress. The NACA Langley 8-Foot HST led the way for testing of high-speed experimental techniques.

9

TOW TANKS NOS. 1 AND 2

Prior to and during World War II, NACA researchers conducted research studies in NACA Langley Tow Tanks Nos. 1 and 2 and in the NACA Langley Impact Basin aimed at finding solutions to problems regarding seaplane hulls and floats. The most common seaplane problem studied in these facilities was the "porpoising" problem experienced in takeoffs and landings by large flying boats. This problem proved to be quite troublesome in that, because of their heavy hulls, the aircraft would bob up and down and, in some cases, skip on the surface of the water, remaining in a dangerous, uncontrollable state. The Navy sought the assistance of NACA Langley to solve these concerning problems in their maritime patrol seaplanes.

Extensive research studies indicated that the addition of a "step" or notch that disrupted the seaplane hull's smooth surface could potentially solve the porpoising and skipping problems. The innovative addition provided two different surfaces, one utilized as the seaplane was churning through the water (during the initial takeoff period and final landing process) and one utilized as the aircraft skimmed along the surface of the water just prior to becoming airborne. Research performed by researchers in the NACA Langley Tow Tank No. 1 also led to the conception of a solution to the spray problem in which water was sprayed onto the propellers and wings of seaplanes. The solution involved the addition of metal strips, which deflected the spray, to the hulls of the seaplanes.

One of the most productive and important Tow Tank No. 1 studies was performed on the design of the Martin PBM Mariner, a large, long-range

Navy flying boat heavily used in the maritime patrol role. As stated by George W. Gray in his book *Frontiers of Flight: The Story of NACA Research* (1948):

> *The PBM Mariner was brought to Langley in its early design stage, and experimental runs in the tank indicated that the hull was too narrow. The beam was eight feet; it was difficult to take off without porpoising; spray was excessive and flung high into propellers and flaps, and the plane could not get off the water with more than 40,000 pounds. As a result of the tank studies, the Mariner was broadened to a ten-foot beam, the line of the step was brought forward several inches, and strips for controlling the spray were built into the forebody. These and other changes were incorporated in the design which reached production as the PBM-3, and the plane was so stable and seaworthy that it was regularly operated at gross weights up to 60,000 pounds.[7]*

In addition to this important seaplane research, the NACA Langley Tow Tank No. 2 was also used to perform invaluable "ditching" studies of scale models of bomber aircraft. Results of these studies and their recommended solutions were later verified in special flight research studies conducted at NACA Langley. These studies were performed on a B-24 heavy bomber model in Tow Tank No. 2. In another scale-model test conducted at NACA

An aerial view of Tow Tank No. 1 in 1938.

During World War II, this model of the legendary "Spruce Goose" flying boat was evaluated in Tow Tank No. 1 for spray effects.

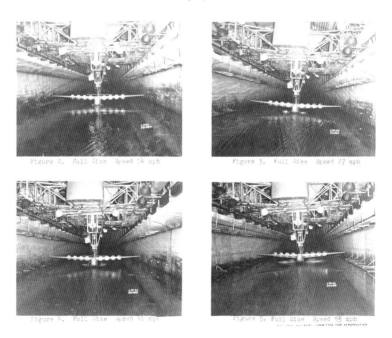

This sequential series of photographs shows the spray effects test of the "Spruce Goose" model in Tow Tank No. 1.

The Martin PBM Mariner was the subject of extensive testing in Tow Tank No. 1 during the war. The Langley Tow Tank tests resulted in important modifications being added to the flying boat's design that enabled it to perform better during the war. *NASA Langley Research Center via Don Loving Collection.*

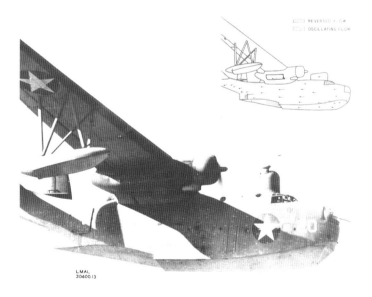

This photo shows aerodynamic flight testing of a PBM to verify results of modifications to the flying boat's hull. Note that wool tufts have been applied to the fuselage to help measure the aerodynamic flow. *NASA Langley Research Center via Don Loving Collection.*

Figure 2. – Flow over a PBM-3 hull at 94 knots, indicated airspeed.

NATIONAL ADVISORY COMMITTEE FOR AERONAUTICS
LANGLEY MEMORIAL AERONAUTICAL LABORATORY - LANGLEY FIELD. VA

NACA Tank No. 2

Description:
Length – 1800 feet
Width – 18 feet
Depth – 6 feet
Carriage Speed – 60 miles per hour

Purpose of Equipment:
To conduct basic hydrodynamic research and to apply the fundamental information obtained to improving the characteristics of seaplanes and flying boats.

Research Projects:
a) Evaluation and improvement of the dynamic stability, resistance, and spray characteristics of dynamic models of specific flying boats.
b) Determination of the effects of various design configurations on the characteristics of seaplanes.
c) To evaluate and improve the ditching characteristics of Army and Navy seaplanes which must operate over water.

Illustrations:
1. Ditching model of the B-29 airplane.
2. Photographs of a ditching of a model of the B-17 airplane with no damage simulated (1-second intervals full-size).
3. XPBB-1 flying boat on which Events-Recorder tests were made by the Open-Water Research Section for correlation with results of tank tests.

NATIONAL ADVISORY COMMITTEE FOR AERONAUTICS
LANGLEY MEMORIAL AERONAUTICAL LABORATORY - LANGLEY FIELD. VA

70

NACA LMAL 41473 12-17-44

Opposite, top: This photo shows aerodynamic flight testing of a PBM flying boat at an airspeed of 94 knots. *NASA Langley Research Center via Don Loving Collection.*

Opposite, bottom: This graphic describes NACA Tow Tank No. 2 and the types of research performed in the facility during World War II.

Above: The scene at Tow Tank No. 2 during a briefing on the undesirable ditching characteristics of a model of the B-24 Liberator bomber. Starr Truscott, chief of the Hydrodynamics Division, and John Dawson, head of Tank No. 2, conduct the briefing.

Early in World War II, the research activities and demands on the original Langley Tow Tank had rapidly increased. The general studies necessary to design seaplanes that would combine freedom from porpoising and skipping, low water resistance and superior performance in the air were directed toward a second Langley towing tank facility, known as Tank No. 2. Tank 2 was declared operational in December 1942, with a basin that was 1,800 feet long, 18 feet wide and 6 feet deep with a 60 mph towing speed capability. In 1943, U.S. military aircraft in the European and Pacific Theaters were experiencing ever-increasing numbers of landings at sea—with attendant losses of aircrews due to loads and drowning—and little guidance regarding piloting techniques or loads to be experienced. The military therefore requested Langley to employ Tank No. 2 for a high-priority research program on ditching at sea. Within Tank 2, models attached to a carriage were accelerated up to a speed of interest and then released to impact the water in the basin with predetermined attitude and configuration. Instrumentation was used to measure pertinent variables such as accelerations and attitudes, while visual recordings were made of the qualitative results. Results of the NACA tests were quickly transmitted to operational units of the Army and Navy. In addition to the tow tank, Langley fabricated the outdoor catapult rig shown here to launch models into the Back River for ditching studies at various sea states. In this picture, a model of the Martin B-26 bomber is in the process of being launched.

Langley, the ditching characteristics of a Martin B-26 Marauder medium bomber model were studied outside of the tow tank along the shore of the nearby Back River. Results of the Langley tow tank and flight research "ditching" studies helped countless Allied bomber aircrews survive water landings when they were forced to ditch their aircraft in waterways around the world.

10

STRUCTURES RESEARCH LABORATORY

The NACA Langley Structures Research Laboratory became operational in October 1940. During the war, researchers in this unique facility made invaluable contributions to the American war effort through the development of advanced aluminum alloys used in the designs of American warplanes. Researchers in this laboratory also performed research regarding the strength and fatigue levels of advanced metals ultimately used in the designs of American military aircraft.

A woman works in the NACA Langley Structures Lab in 1943.

11

MODEL SHOPS

W hen analyzing the many contributions of NACA Langley to the achievement of Allied victory in World War II, the importance of the role of the NACA Langley Model Shops should not be overlooked. Workers in these shops built a multitude of scale models that were ultimately tested in Langley's PRT, FST, Spin Tunnel, 16-Foot HST, 8-Foot HST and Tow Tank No. 1. Tests of these models resulted in modifications to military aircraft designs that proved to be immense in importance and led to the achievement of Allied victory in the war.

A team of women work on a flying boat model in the NACA Langley Model Shop in 1943. *NASA Langley Research Center.*

PART II

. . . .

FLIGHT RESEARCH

During World War II, the NACA Langley Flight Research Division made numerous crucial contributions to the Allied war effort. Aircraft development projects were dramatically increased at the onset of the war. As a result, a corresponding dramatic increase in workload was experienced by NACA Langley's staff. The tremendous increase in the number of aerodynamically enhanced designs emerging from Langley FST tests meant that there was a need to flight-prove the aircraft to verify the validity of proposed design improvements.

From the beginning of America's entry into and throughout the duration of World War II, Langley Flight Research Division personnel were highly engaged in the verification of drag reduction and inlet recovery projects and the testing of propeller efficiency and longitudinal stability. The Flight Research Division also assessed the roll performance of fighter aircraft and the validity of the all-moving horizontal stabilizers concept. As a result of this workload explosion, the NACA decided to update the requirements for all military aircraft.

Langley Flight Research pilots participated in evaluations of foreign military aircraft over the course of the war. The foreign military aircraft evaluations yielded invaluable information concerning both Allied and Axis aircraft performance. The Flight Research Division also performed flight research studies of advanced airfoils, including the revolutionary NACA laminar airfoil. Langley pilots achieved another milestone during the war when they flight-evaluated the first practical helicopter, the Sikorsky HNS-1 Hoverfly.

Interestingly, NACA Langley and the Army conducted a flight research study during the war that called for the ditching of a Consolidated B-24D Liberator in the James River. The study yielded invaluable information for heavy bomber aircrews, which operated their aircraft over the oceans in both the European and Pacific Theaters.

During the course of the war, fighter pilots began to encounter compressibility problems with their aircraft as they pushed the limits of their piston-engine fighters. One of these fighters encountering compressibility problems happened to be the Lockheed P-38 Lightning. NACA Langley engineers and pilots undertook a special effort to conduct flight research studies in a speed range in excess of the limits of the fighter aircraft experiencing this phenomenon, known as the transonic flight regime (speeds approaching and passing through the sound barrier).

Two methods for studying transonic phenomena were conceived by Langley scientists and engineers. The first method became known as the wing flow method and was devised by Dr. Robert Gilruth. This method involved the installation of different wing model types on a special wing test section of a P-51D Mustang and forcing the airplane into a steep dive. The second method called for the dropping of bomb drop models from underwing pylons on heavy bombers. The bomb drop models reached transonic speeds in free-fall and were tracked via telemetering.

Throughout the war, it was a vital requirement that Langley pilots become proficient and master flight in a variety of fighters, dive bombers, torpedo bombers and heavy bombers. They trained via a control link flight simulator.

The NACA Langley Flight Research Division utilized two hangars for flight research operations during the war. The division was composed of five primary flight research pilots and supporting staff, including engineers, mechanics and administrative personnel.

Melvin Gough served as the chief test pilot and head of NACA Flight Operations at Langley during World War II. Gough happened to be the first NACA engineering test pilot. Gough held a bachelor of science (BS) degree in aeronautical engineering from Johns Hopkins University. Several years after the war, during the advent of America's space program, Gough took a leadership position at NASA's Cape Canaveral Station (now Kennedy Space Center) in Florida.

Herb Hoover served as second in command of NACA Flight Operations at Langley during World War II. Following the war,

An aerial view of the flight research subject lineup at NACA Langley in 1944. Visible at the top right of the picture are the two large NACA Langley flight research hangars in the background. This photo illustrates the large quantity of flight research projects undertaken by the LMAL during World War II.

he became the first civilian test pilot to fly the Bell XS-1 (wearing NACA markings) past the sound barrier.

Jack Reeder came to work at NACA Langley in 1938, first serving as an aeronautical engineer assigned to the FST. During the war, the NACA experienced a shortage of test pilots, and Reeder took advantage of the opportunity, transferring to the Flight Research Division in 1942. He became a prolific test pilot during the war, serving as the primary test pilot on a multitude of aircraft projects. He was also an engineering test pilot, having earned a BS in aeronautical engineering from the University of Michigan. Reeder worked for the NACA/NASA for forty-two years and retired in 1980. He test-flew a total of 235 aircraft and rotorcraft during his career. He was also the agency's first helicopter pilot. Many of his peers considered him to have been the agency's finest test pilot.

Opposite, top: An interior view of one of the NACA Langley flight research hangars in 1945. Visible in the foreground is the Sikorsky HNS-1 helicopter flight-tested by NACA Langley engineering test pilot John P. "Jack" Reeder in March of the same year. *NARA*.

Opposite, bottom: NACA Langley test pilots Jack Reeder, Herb Hoover, Mel Gough and Bill Gray pose in front of the North American XP-51 Mustang for a publicity photo at NACA Langley in 1943. These four men served as the LMAL's primary flight research pilots during the war. *NASA Langley Research Center via Larry Loftin Collection*.

Above: Primary NACA Langley test pilots (*from left to right*) Melvin Gough, Herbert Hoover, John P. "Jack" Reeder, Stefan A. Cavallo and William E. Gray Jr. pose in front of a Republic P-47D Thunderbolt fighter for a publicity photo. *NASA Langley Research Center via Jack Reeder Collection*.

Stefan Cavallo also served as flight research test pilot at NACA Langley during the war. He made significant test-piloting contributions to numerous flight research projects.

Bill Gray was the fifth primary flight research pilot at NACA Langley during World War II. Like Cavallo, he also made significant test-piloting contributions to a plethora of flight research projects.

12

FIGHTERS

During World War II, the NACA Langley Flight Research Division flight-tested practically every fighter aircraft in the American military aircraft arsenal. The division also flight-tested some of the most prominent fighter aircraft in the British Royal Air Force's (RAF's) fighter aircraft arsenal. The majority of the American fighter flight test programs involved the verification of wind-tunnel test results.

Brewster F2A Buffalo

The Brewster F2A Buffalo was a short-range fighter used by the U.S. Navy and Marine Corps at the beginning of World War II. The Buffalo was a pre–World War II fighter design that, when first rolled off the assembly line, suffered from aerodynamic drag problems. Extensive testing, including drag cleanup studies, of the prototype aircraft, the XF2A, in Langley's FST led to dramatic gains in the aircraft's overall aerodynamic performance. These gains were confirmed through extensive flight research studies of production variants of the Buffalo, conducted at NACA Langley.

A Brewster F2A-2 Buffalo, piloted by a Langley test pilot, in flight over Hampton, Virginia, in 1942. The Buffalo was used in flight research at Langley to verify modifications made to the aircraft's design as a result of Full-Scale Wind Tunnel drag cleanup studies performed on the aircraft. *NASA Langley Research Center via Don Loving Collection.*

CURTISS P-40 TOMAHAWK/WARHAWK

Similar to the Buffalo, the Curtiss P-40 Tomahawk prototype, the XP-40, was also a prewar fighter design and suffered from aerodynamic drag problems. When the aircraft design emerged from NACA Langley FST drag cleanup studies, it boasted a top speed increase of 42 miles per hour.[8] This result was later confirmed in flight tests of U.S. Army Air Corp/Army Air Force production model P-40s at NACA Langley. The Tomahawk was also the subject of flight qualities testing at NACA Langley. These studies revealed that although the aircraft's flying qualities were found to be adequate, there were heavy aileron control forces. The aircraft also possessed "poor" stalling characteristics. As stated by NACA Langley engineer W. Hewitt Phillips, "The airplane had a particularly bad tendency to ground loop, which was found to be caused by asymmetrical stalling of the wing in the three-point attitude. This problem was cured by extending the tail-wheel strut so that the airplane remained unstalled on the ground."[9]

The Curtiss P-40 fighter was the subject of extensive study prior to and during the early years of World War II at NACA Langley. Here, a P-40B Tomahawk awaits drag-reduction flight research studies at Langley.

A Curtiss P-40 with enhanced wing leading-edge "blister" installation at NACA Langley. Research performed at Langley led to the modification of the aircraft's fairings under the wing that housed the landing gear. This modification led to improved aerodynamic performance and was incorporated in the Army's Tomahawk fleet. *NASA Langley Research Center via Don Loving Collection.*

A Curtiss P-40E Warhawk, with original tail configuration, at NACA Langley on July 13, 1942. *NASA Langley Research Center via Don Loving Collection.*

A Curtiss P-40E Warhawk, with modified tail configuration, at NACA Langley later in 1942. The tail configuration modification was the result of research performed at Langley that ultimately improved the aircraft's stability and control. *NASA Langley Research Center via Don Loving Collection.*

A Curtiss P-40F Warhawk at NACA Langley in January 1944. *NASA Langley Research Center via Don Loving Collection.*

A Curtiss P-40K Warhawk, with original tail configuration, at NACA Langley in 1942. *NASA Langley Research Center via Don Loving Collection.*

A Curtiss P-40K Warhawk, with modified tail configuration, at NACA Langley in 1943. The tail configuration modification was the result of research performed at Langley that ultimately improved the aircraft's stability and control. *NASA Langley Research Center via Don Loving Collection.*

Engineering test pilot Jack Reeder boards a Curtiss P-40F Warhawk before takeoff on a flight research mission at Langley in October 1943. Reeder arrived at work for Langley in 1938 and was tasked as working as an aeronautical engineer in the Full-Scale Wind Tunnel. Due to a scarcity of test pilots, Reeder transferred to the Flight Research Division in 1942. He went on to serve a distinguished forty-two-year career with NACA/ NASA Langley and retired in 1980. He was perhaps the most accomplished NACA/ NASA engineering test pilot, having test-flown 235 types of aircraft and rotorcraft. *NASA Langley Research Center via Larry Loftin Collection.*

BELL YP-39/P-39 AIRACOBRA

Much like the XF2A and the XP-40, the Bell XP-39, prototype of the famous Airacobra fighter aircraft series, was a pre–World War II fighter design that similarly suffered from aerodynamic drag problems. The XP-39 also underwent extensive drag cleanup studies in the Langley FST, emerging with significantly enhanced performance characteristics. This was also confirmed through flight testing at NACA Langley of a YP-39 Airacobra prototype as well as production variants of the aircraft in service with the U.S. Army Air Corps / U.S. Army Air Forces (USAAF).

Top: The Bell YP-39 Airacobra in its original condition at NACA Langley in 1941. *NASA Langley Research Center via Don Loving Collection.*

Bottom: The Bell YP-39 Airacobra after undergoing Langley-inspired modifications at NACA Langley. Note the propeller wake survey rakes on the fuselage sides of the aircraft. *NARA.*

A Bell P-39 Airacobra, with Langley test pilot Herb Hoover at the controls, in flight over Langley in early 1943. *NARA.*

GRUMMAN F4F WILDCAT

Prior to World War II, the Grumman XF4F Wildcat (prototype of the famous "Wildcat" series) underwent drag cleanup studies in the Langley FST that led to significant enhancements in the aircraft's aerodynamic performance. Production variants of the Wildcat were later flight-tested at NACA Langley to confirm these enhancements while studying the stability and control characteristics of these aircraft.

CURTISS XP-42

In 1943, NACA Langley conducted flight evaluations of the revolutionary Army Curtiss XP-42, a developmental variant of the pre–World War II Curtiss P-36 Hawk that incorporated a new engine cowling developed by the NACA as well as an all-moving horizontal stabilizer that significantly improved maneuverability.

A Grumman F4F-3 Wildcat awaits flight research studies at Langley immediately prior to World War II. Flight research was performed on the Wildcat to verify results of modifications to the aircraft's design inspired by Langley's FST drag cleanup studies. *NASA Langley Research Center via Don Loving Collection.*

A Navy Grumman F4F-3 Wildcat awaits flight research studies at Langley in early 1942.

A Navy General Motors FM-2 Wildcat awaits flight research studies at Langley in late World War II. *NASA Langley Research Center via Don Loving Collection.*

The Curtiss XP-42 in flight above Langley in 1942. The aircraft featured an all-moving horizontal stabilizer concept. The airplane also featured special aerodynamically designed engine cowls.

VOUGHT XF4U-1/F4U-1 CORSAIR

In late 1941, the Langley Flight Research Division conducted flight evaluations of the prototype of a new Navy fighter, the Vought XF4U-1 Corsair. The Corsair would go on to become one of the finest American fighters used in combat during World War II. Prior to its entry into mass production, results obtained from wind-tunnel studies, including drag cleanup studies, at NACA Langley led to numerous modifications in the aircraft's design that yielded major gains in aerodynamic performance and operational capability. Phillips later elaborated on flying qualities flight research studies of the Corsair:

> *The elevator control forces in turns were found to be desirably light, but the aileron forces in high-speed rolls were heavy, resulting in sluggish response. The rudder force variation with speed for trim in high-speed dives and strafing runs was large, resulting in difficulty in holding the sights on an aim point. Control forces in the carrier approach condition had an unstable variation with speed, a common condition that does not have a very adverse effect on the flying qualities.*[10]

The Vought-Sikorsky XF4U-1, prototype of the legendary Corsair fighter series, awaits flight testing at Langley during the early years of World War II.

A Chance Vought F4U-1 Corsair awaits flight testing at Langley in 1942. This early version of the Corsair featured a "birdcage" canopy. Langley test pilots discovered numerous design problems with the aircraft, including poor piloting vision from a low pilot's seat and a troublesome tail wheel configuration. NACA Langley's recommendations led to raising the seat and the tail wheel. The problems identified by NACA Langley plagued the airplane's Navy carrier trials. But the aircraft was subsequently modified per NACA Langley's recommendations and eventually passed its carrier trials.

Not all of the Corsair flight tests went well at NACA Langley, as recalled by NACA Langley primary engineering test pilot Jack Reeder many years later:

In 1943 I had my first real emergency after transferring to the NACA piloting staff. I was flying an F4U-1 Corsair, one of the early versions which had the low cockpit and seat, the "birdcage" canopy and the low tailwheel. Also, the cowl-flap opening extended over the top of the fuselage ahead of the canopy. A hydraulic torquemeter, using engine oil, was installed for power measurements. Suddenly, while flying northwest of Newport News at about 4000 feet, a torquemeter pressure line on the engine face, carrying oil at 400 psi broke. A thick blanket of oil rolled over the windshield and airplane. I had to open the canopy to see outside. The cockpit and I were soon bathed with oil, and I had to raise my goggles

Langley's flight research organization during the war achieved an outstanding safety record, despite the rigors of evaluating a large number of prototypes, variants of in-service aircraft and experimental versions of all types of airplanes. Famous Langley pilot Jack Reeder was involved in a harrowing experience during a test flight in the local area of an early Navy F4U-1 Corsair fighter in August 1943. The engine experienced a major oil leak, coating the entire canopy and forward fuselage with a blanket of oil. Reeder quickly opened the cockpit for better vision and noted that the wing was covered with oil, preventing him from bailing out of the airplane. He was coated with oil and had to raise his flight goggles to have any visibility at all. During his challenging emergency landing at Langley Field, he had to keep his head in the cockpit to avoid being completely blinded by the oil. During the approach to landing without forward visibility, Reeder used his peripheral vision and the tails of B-24s parked on the side of the runway for cues that enabled his touchdown. This photograph shows the extensive oil slick that coated Reeder's aircraft during the test flight.

to see at all. I decided everything was too slippery to bail out safely, so I headed for Langley to land. Observers thought I was on fire. As I leaned to the left edge of the cockpit to see a little better for the approach, flying oil and the wind blast made it difficult to determine my orientation. I tried to wipe and pull down my goggles again but the wind took them away. The last time I saw the runway was on the base leg. I had to prejudge the turn into final and the proper descent path, while keeping my head well inside the edge of the windshield to prevent my left eye from being closed by the wind. As I approached the threshold, I judged height and flare distance by the tails of B-24's on the adjacent taxiway waiting for takeoff. Touchdown

Right: A close-up view of the oil slick–coated engine cowling and forward fuselage of Reeder's F4U-1 Corsair.

Below: A Chance Vought F4U-1D Corsair awaits flight testing at Langley. *NASA Langley Research Center via Don Loving Collection.*

was on the runway, wheels first with tail slightly low and with a slight impact. The airplane began to bounce (the very reason the F4U-1 did not qualify for carrier operation originally). The lower I pushed the nose, the more severe the bounce. I then discovered that I had left the throttle cracked and the bouncing stopped as soon as I closed the throttle fully. I stopped on the runway, but getting down from the high cockpit, using all the little steps provided, was hazardous because of the total oil slick. I realized I had not become nervous or upset—too busy![11]

One of Reeder's former NASA Langley colleagues later recalled a humorous event that transpired when Reeder was test-flying the early Corsair variant. "I remember Jack Reeder talking about flight testing the F4U Corsair. One day he was working through the flight card on a test flight and he thought he would test the relief tube. As he tested the tube, it blew back at him and he emphatically noted on the flight card: 'Change location of relief tube exit.'"[12]

REPUBLIC P-47 THUNDERBOLT

In 1942, NACA Langley conducted flight research studies of a new fighter that was used quite effectively in both the European and Pacific Theaters by the USAAF, the Republic P-47 Thunderbolt. Flight tests of a Republic P-47B Razorback were conducted at Langley in 1942 to study the loads and maneuverability characteristics of the aircraft. The aircraft was heavily armored and later excelled as an escort fighter for American heavy bombers and as a ground attack aircraft.

Jack Reeder had the opportunity to test-fly one of the final versions of the Thunderbolt produced, the P-47D-30. The P-47D-30 was used in combat in Europe in early 1945. Reeder elaborated on the aircraft's flight characteristics in the following excerpt from an official NACA technical note:

Flight tests have been made to determine the longitudinal stability and control and stalling characteristics of an F-47D-30 airplane. The results of these tests show the airplane to be unstable with stick free in any power-on condition even at the most forward center-of-gravity position tested. At the rearward center-of-gravity position, elevator-force reversals were experienced in turns at low speeds, and the elevator-force variations with acceleration

In 1942, NACA Langley performed load and maneuverability flight research studies using this Republic P-47B Razorback Thunderbolt, an early variant of the famous Thunderbolt series. The Thunderbolt later performed exceptionally as an escort fighter and fighter bomber in the ground attack role during the war.

A P-47C Thunderbolt awaits flight testing at NACA Langley during World War II. *NASA Langley Research Center via Larry Loftin Collection.*

A P-47D awaits flight research studies at NACA Langley in 1944. *NASA Langley Research Center via Don Loving Collection.*

Engineering test pilot Jack Reeder piloting a Republic P-47D-30 above the James River in early 1945. This aircraft was used in flight research studies aimed at evaluating the propeller characteristics for various propeller blade configurations. Note the propeller wake survey rakes on the forward fuselage of the aircraft. *NASA Langley Research Center via Don Loving Collection.*

A Republic P-47D-28 awaits propeller efficiency, handling and performance flight testing at NACA Langley in 1945.

were low at all the other speeds tested. Ample stall warning was afforded in all the conditions tested and the stalling characteristics were satisfactory except in the approach and wave-off conditions.[13]

NORTH AMERICAN XP-51 / P-51B / P-51D / P-51H MUSTANG

Perhaps NACA Langley's most significant World War II flight research studies were those performed on the North American P-51 Mustang. All variants of the Mustang were all-time favorites among the NACA Langley test pilots. The aircraft made use of the revolutionary NACA laminar flow airfoil, which was one of the primary factors that made it an extremely effective fighter and piston-engine "game changer" in the war. As later stated by Reeder, the aircraft "was a 'very fine flying machine' and one of the best fighters he had ever flown."[14] He later recalled that "when the XP-51 (the Mustang prototype) came out, it could fly 30 mph faster than any comparable fighter plane of its time."[15]

Initial flight evaluations of the XP-51 began at Langley in late 1941. Later, Reeder was selected to perform XP-51 flight evaluations following aileron system modifications that were made at the recommendation of the NACA. The NACA modifications significantly enhanced the aircraft's control and maneuverability. Reeder test-flew XP-51 #4 (serial number 41-38) in 1944 and noted the superb stability and control characteristics of the aircraft. This aircraft is currently part of the collection of the Air Venture Museum of the Experimental Aircraft Association at Oshkosh, Wisconsin.

Reeder and other NACA Langley test pilots also test-flew Mustang production variants, including the P-51B, P-51D and P-51H. Reeder became the lead test pilot for a flight research study of the P-51H. According to a NACA Research Memorandum for the USAAF:

> *Flight tests have been made to determine the longitudinal stability and control and stalling characteristics of a North American P-51H airplane. The results indicate that the airplane has satisfactory longitudinal stability in all the flight conditions tested at normal loadings up to 25,000 feet*

The North American XP-51 Mustang prototype awaits flight testing at NACA Langley in 1941. The P-51 was the subject of extensive wind-tunnel and flight research at Langley that enhanced the aerodynamic performance of the ultimate piston-engine fighter "game changer" of World War II. With Langley-inspired elements and modifications to its design, the Mustang ultimately enabled the Allies to attain air superiority over the Axis in the skies above Europe during the war.

The cannon-armed Army North American XP-51 Mustang at NACA Langley in 1941. *NASA Langley Research Center via Larry Loftin Collection.*

The XP-51 at Langley on September 1, 1943. *NASA Langley Research Center via Don Loving Collection.*

A side view of the XP-51 at Langley in 1943. *NASA Langley Research Center via Don Loving Collection.*

A side view of a P-51B at Langley on September 1, 1943. *NASA Langley Research Center via Don Loving Collection.*

A NACA Langley test pilot puts a P-51B Mustang through its paces during a flight research mission aimed at measuring the effectiveness of the revolutionary NACA laminar flow airfoil in 1943. Note the wing glove, which has been fitted over the wing section and the survey rake positioned on the trailing edge of the wing. The survey rake measured the wake characteristics of the wing section. *NARA.*

Another view of the P-51B previously pictured.

Above: A North American P-51D Mustang awaits flight research studies at NACA Langley in early 1945. Langley test pilots flew this aircraft in handling and performance studies. The aircraft was also test-flown to evaluate its bubbletop canopy. *NASA Langley Research Center via Larry Loftin Collection.*

Left: Legendary Langley test pilot Jack Reeder boards a P-51D Mustang prior to performing a flight research study in 1945. The Mustang was Reeder's all-time favorite aircraft to fly. *NASA Langley Research Center via Larry Loftin Collection.*

Langley test pilot Jack Reeder performs a flight research mission in a P-51H over the James River in 1945. *NASA Langley Research Center via Larry Loftin Collection.*

altitude. At Mach numbers above 0.7, the elevator push force required for longitudinal trim decreased somewhat because of compressibility effects. The elevator stick force per g in accelerated turns at the forward center-of-gravity position of 24 percent mean aerodynamic chord above 250 miles per hour was in excess of the required limits at both 5,000 and 25,000 feet altitude. The longitudinal-trim-force changes due to flaps and power were small, but the rudder-trim-force change with power change was high. The stalling characteristics in all the conditions tested were satisfactory….There was ample stall warning and recovery was always normal and prompt.[16]

GRUMMAN F6F-3 HELLCAT

In early 1943, the NACA Langley Flight Research Division was tasked with performing flight evaluations of a new advanced carrier-borne fighter for the Navy, the Grumman F6F-3 Hellcat. Among the many Hellcat flight evaluations conducted at Langley were performance and handling tests, which yielded modifications to the airplane's lateral controls. These lateral control modifications were ultimately incorporated in later Hellcat variants, and this led to enhanced overall performance. Flight investigations into the stalling characteristics of the Hellcat were also conducted and documented by NACA Langley. The Hellcat would go on to account for a majority of all U.S. Navy aerial victories registered in the Pacific.

As later stated by Laurence K. Loftin Jr., a former director of aeronautics at NASA Langley Research Center:

> *Few changes were made in this outstanding aircraft in its operational lifetime, and by March 1945, the production rate reached 605 aircraft per month with an unbelievable unit price of $35,000. Certainly, the Hellcat was one of the most successful fighters of the war, and one that required the least modification with service use of any such aircraft ever produced. The F6F-3 investigated by the NACA was the number 2 production aircraft. The only criticism of the F6F-3 was in relation to the lateral controls which were thought to be somewhat heavy. This was corrected in a modification which appeared on the F6F-5, an advanced version of the Hellcat.*[17]

Jack Reeder drew the assignment of performing the Hellcat longitudinal stability and control characteristics flight studies. The results were later revealed in a NACA report to the Navy that was coauthored by Reeder:

> *At the request of the Bureau of Aeronautics, Navy Department, flight measurements were made of the handling qualities of an F6F-3 airplane. Thirty flights were made covering the period from February 1 to May 15, 1944.*[18]
>
> *In general, the pilots were favorably impressed with the longitudinal stability and control of the F6F-3 airplane. They considered it an easy airplane to fly. The control forces in abrupt and steady maneuvers were satisfactory. Also, the airplane was very easy to land. The results of the tests described herein showed the following details concerning the longitudinal stability and control of the F6F-3 airplane.*
>
> *1. The short-period longitudinal oscillations of the F6F-3 airplane were completely damped within one cycle.*
> *2. The neutral point (stick fixed) in the gliding condition varied from 36 percent mean aerodynamic chord at a lift coefficient of 0.2 to 39 percent mean aerodynamic chord at a lift coefficient of 1.0. Application of rated*

power (climbing condition) had a destabilizing effect above a lift coefficient of 0.4 which increased with increase in lift coefficient. In this condition the neutral point was located at 31.5 percent mean aerodynamic chord at a C_L of 1.0. At lift coefficients below 0.4, application of power appeared to have a small stabilizing effect.

3. The use of flaps had a destabilizing effect. The stick-fixed neutral point in the landing condition varied from 35 percent mean aerodynamic chord at a C_L of 0.8 to 37 percent mean aerodynamic chord at a C_L of 1.4. The effects of power and flaps combined to make the wave-off the least stable condition tested.

4. The stability with stick free was less than stick fixed. The difference between stick-free and stick-fixed stability increased with increase in lift coefficient.

5. The stick force per g in maneuvers was satisfactory (3 to 8 pounds per g) at 3000 feet altitude for a center-of-gravity range between 29.9 and 33.2 percent mean aerodynamic chord. The desirable center-of-gravity range at 20,000 feet altitude lies between 26.6 and 30.5 percent mean aerodynamic chord.

6. The elevator provided adequate control in takeoff at the most rearward center of gravity tested.

7. The elevator power in landing was sufficient to effect three-point contact with the center of gravity aft of 21.5 percent mean aerodynamic chord.

8. The longitudinal trim changes due to power and flaps were within the specified limits.

9. The elevator trim tab was sufficiently powerful to trim the airplane as desired throughout the speed range in all flight conditions except below 120 miles per hour in the landing condition.[19]

In addition to these Hellcat flight research studies, the Bureau of Aeronautics requested that the NACA conduct flight investigations to determine the Hellcat's stalling characteristics. Jack Reeder once again performed these flight investigations. He summarized the results and his conclusions in the following excerpt from the final NACA report:

1. Stall warnings existed in steady flight for the gliding, climbing, and landing conditions in the form of increased vibration, a duct howl in the power-off conditions, and gentle buffeting. The buffeting is not a reliable warning as it is obtained only if the stall approach is very slow. No stall warning existed for the approach or wave-off conditions.

Side view of a Grumman F6F-3 Hellcat awaiting performance and handling flight tests at NACA Langley in early 1943. *NASA Langley Research Center via Don Loving Collection.*

Flight tests of the F6F-3 at Langley inspired modifications to the airplane's lateral controls, which were added to later Hellcat variants. The modifications led to enhanced overall performance. *NASA Langley Research Center via Larry Loftin Collection.*

2. The initial roll-off was mild in most cases and could be checked by the use of ailerons and rudder. In cases where little or no control was used after the initial roll-off, mild rolling, and pitching oscillations set in and continued through the stall.

3. In accelerated flight, stall warning was afforded by buffeting of the entire airplane. The resultant pitching and rolling oscillations, as well as the final roll-off, were mild and easily controllable.[20]

LOCKHEED YP-38 LIGHTNING

During the early portion of World War II, NACA Langley performed flight research studies on the second Lockheed P-38 Lightning prototype, the YP-38. The airplane was extensively studied for drag reduction or "cleanup" in the Langley FST. Results from these studies yielded modifications to the aircraft that were verified and validated through flight testing at Langley. Interestingly, pilots first noticed the high-speed compressibility dilemma in the YP-38, which led to Langley undertaking an extensive transonic flight research program toward the end of World War II.

BELL P-63 KINGCOBRA

NACA Langley undertook the task of flight evaluating an advanced version of the Bell P-39 Airacobra, the P-63 Kingcobra, in late 1943. These flight research efforts were intended to lead to enhancements of the airplane's performance and handling characteristics. Through these flight studies, NACA Langley test pilots found that the addition of a taller vertical tail significantly enhanced stability and control.

GRUMMAN XF8F-1 BEARCAT

In early 1945, NACA Langley performed flight research studies on the outstanding Grumman XF8F-1 Bearcat (prototype of the Bearcat series), intended to serve as a replacement for the famous Hellcat. While production

The Lockheed YP-38 Lightning, the second prototype aircraft of the famous Lightning series, awaits flight testing at Langley early in World War II. Langley performed flight tests in the aircraft to verify modifications made to the airplane's design after it underwent Langley FST drag cleanup studies.

A Bell P-63 Kingcobra awaits performance and handling characteristics flight research studies at Langley in 1943. *NASA Langley Research Center via Don Loving Collection.*

Pictured on the top is the P-63 in its original design configuration. Pictured below is the P-63 with Langley research–inspired design modifications incorporated in the aircraft's design. Note the tall vertical tail for improved stability and control. *NASA Langley Research Center via Don Loving Collection.*

A modified P-63 on a flight research mission near Langley in late 1943. Note the survey rakes positioned on the forward fuselage to measure propeller wake flow. *NARA.*

NACA Langley chief test pilot and head of the Flight Research Division, Mel Gough, boards the Bell P-63 Kingcobra in late 1943. The aircraft has tufts of wool attached to show airflow behavior while in flight. Gough was LMAL's first engineering test pilot. *NASA Langley Research Center via Larry Loftin Collection.*

of the Bearcat commenced in early 1945, the aircraft never saw combat during the war. At Langley, test pilots performed stability and control studies in the aircraft. These studies led to a production modification to the aircraft's vertical tail in which the tail was made taller than in the initial prototype. This enhancement led to better directional stability and control in the aircraft.

Langley's flight research work on the Bearcat was best summarized in a paper written by Jack Reeder and Bearcat project engineer H.L. Crane:

This paper presents the results of flight tests to determine the lateral and directional stability and control characteristics of the Grumman F8F-1 airplane with three vertical-tail configurations. The data presented herein have no bearing on the performance characteristics of the airplane, which were not measured but which were considered to be exceptionally good. The conclusions reached regarding the lateral and directional stability and control characteristics may be summarized as follows:

1. It was found that the directional stability was poor with the production vertical tail. Addition of a 12-inch extension to the vertical fin and rudder produced a desirable improvement in directional stability and control characteristics. However, further enlargement of the vertical tail would be required to make the directional stability satisfactory in all respects.

2. There was a tendency for the rudder control force to overbalance at large angles of right sideslip with the modified vertical tails. There was no such tendency with the production tail configuration which included a dorsal fin. It was concluded that the dorsal fin should have been retained on the modified vertical tails.

3. The aileron control characteristics were better than those of many comparable airplanes which have been tested. However, the ailerons did not satisfy the Navy requirements for satisfactory flying qualities with regard to either control forces or rolling effectiveness.

4. The power of the rudder trimming tab proved to be inadequate and the tab should be enlarged and/or be provided with an increased deflection range.[21]

The Grumman XF8F-1 Bearcat at Langley in 1945. *NASA Langley Research Center via Don Loving Collection.*

Langley test pilot William Gray Jr. pilots the Grumman XF8F-1 on a flight research mission in early 1945. *NASA Langley Research Center via Larry Loftin Collection.*

Hawker Hurricane Mk. IIA

In late 1941, NACA Langley conducted flight evaluations of a RAF interceptor veteran of the Battle of Britain, the Hawker Hurricane Mk.IIA. The NACA Hurricane flight research studies were aimed at eliminating drag and stall problems exacerbated by the British procedure of placing canvas-type fabric over the gun ports of the airplane. The NACA flight studies resulted in a drastic decline in the number of British Hurricane incidents. Flying qualities flight research studies of the Hurricane conducted at NACA Langley revealed that while the airplane's flying qualities were found to be adequate, its inadequacies included high-speed heavy aileron forces and substantial control friction. These findings were shared with Hawker.

Supermarine Spitfire Mk. II

In early 1942, NACA Langley conducted flight evaluations of another superb RAF interceptor veteran of the Battle of Britain, the Supermarine Spitfire Mk. II. The NACA Spitfire flight research studies were also aimed at studying the gun port covering effects. In addition, the maneuverability and handling qualities of the aircraft were studied. NACA Langley flying qualities flight research studies of the Spitfire Mk. II revealed that the aircraft generally possessed excellent maneuverability and handling characteristics; however, it was found that the airplane experienced substantial aileron forces and was sluggish in rolls at high speeds. These findings were shared with Supermarine.

Supermarine Spitfire Mk. VII

In late 1944, NACA Langley performed flight research studies in a high-altitude variant of the famous Spitfire, the Supermarine Spitfire Mk. VII. Jack Reeder was involved in these studies. Reeder test-flew the Spitfire Mk. VII to evaluate what aerodynamic effects were produced when canvas coverings were placed over the airplane's outer wing gun ports. This was a standard World War II practice that the British applied to their Spitfire and Hawker Hurricane fighter aircraft that inhibited the accumulation of dirt

A British Hawker Hurricane Mk. IIA at Langley in late 1941.

A British Supermarine Spitfire Mk. II at Langley in early 1942. *NASA Langley Research Center via Larry Loftin Collection.*

A British Supermarine Spitfire Mk. VII at Langley in late 1944.

and mud in the ports. When firing the guns, the cannon shells or machine gun bullets pierced the canvas and did not adversely affect their trajectory. The practice did ultimately produce drag, and as stated by W. Hewitt Phillips, a prominent NACA Langley engineer at the time, "some of the Spitfires stalled in flight after firing their cannons/machine guns due to the rough protrusions left on the leading edge of the wings."[22] The results of the NACA Langley Spitfire flight research studies ultimately enabled the British to eliminate this problem for the remainder of the war. The Spitfire Mk. VII was also evaluated at NACA Langley for handling and performance characteristics and test-flown in pilot familiarization studies.

CAPTURED JAPANESE MITSUBISHI A6M2 ZERO

In early 1943, NACA Langley conducted static and FST evaluations of a captured Japanese Mitsubishi A6M2 Zero. The aircraft underwent instrumentation outfitting at Langley before being flight-tested by the Navy. These flight tests ultimately revealed the secrets of the Zero's superiority during the early years of the war. Consequently, American combat pilots were able to devise new tactics that enabled them to capitalize on the Zero's weaknesses. American fighter airplane manufacturers were also able to modify the designs of their late-war fighter aircraft to the extent that they dominated the Zero in the last years of the war.

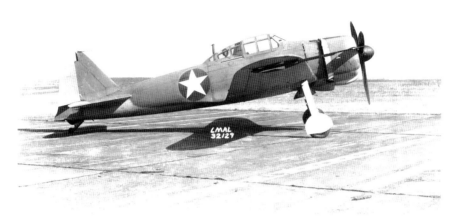

A true wolf in sheep's clothing, this Japanese Mitsubishi Zero was the first airworthy Zero captured by the United States in the war, having been shot down during a raid in 1942 on an Army outpost at Alaska's Aleutian archipelago. It was salvaged and refurbished by the Navy, painted in U.S. colors and insignia and flown on the West Coast for mock dogfights against first-line U.S. aircraft to develop tactics to use against the Zero. Results of the successful evaluations were quickly transmitted to front-line units, an action regarded by many historians as a critical factor in success during the war in the Pacific. In March 1943, the Navy requested that Langley flight researchers instrument the airplane for quantitative evaluations by Navy pilots at Naval Air Station Anacostia in Washington, D.C. The Zero was flown to Langley by a Navy pilot and arrived on March 8. During its stay, Langley's chief of aerodynamics, Elton Miller, and the head of the Full-Scale Tunnel Section, Abe Silverstein, were granted permission to test the aircraft in the Full-Scale Tunnel. After these tests, the airplane was returned to the Langley hangar and flight instrumentation was installed by Langley's flight organization. The Zero then left for NAS Anacostia, where the Navy-simulated combat flights were flown. *NASA Langley Research Center via Larry Loftin Collection.*

BOMBERS

The NACA Langley Flight Research division also flight-tested and evaluated examples of almost the entire U.S. bomber fleet during World War II. The Langley Flight Research Division conducted important flight research studies regarding stability and control, handling characteristics, water impact crew survivability, radar bombing and special transonic bomb drop. Many of these studies enabled the Allies to gain an edge over the Axis in operating light attack, medium and heavy bombers during the war.

DIVE BOMBERS

Curtiss SB2C Helldiver

NACA Langley conducted extensive flight studies of the Navy's replacement for the venerable Douglas SBD Dauntless dive bomber, the Curtiss SB2C-1 Helldiver. In 1943, NACA Langley test pilot Herbert Hoover performed control and maneuverability flight research studies of the Helldiver. In 1944, Jack Reeder performed test flights in the Helldiver to evaluate modifications made to the airplane's elevators and wing-tip slots.

The modifications made to the Helldiver's elevator system were described in detail by Reeder and engineer Maurice D. White in the following excerpt from the official NACA Memorandum Report on the subject:

Three sets of elevators with various combinations of section contour, balancing tabs, bobweights, and control-system mechanical advantage were tested on an SB2C-1 airplane in an attempt to improve the elevator control-

force characteristics in maneuvers. An arrangement was developed which with a 3-pound bobweight gave a variation of maneuvering stick forces of 6 to 18 pounds per g acceleration over the operating center-of-gravity range of 33.2 to 23.8 percent mean aerodynamic chord; this arrangement consisted of elevators having a nose contour less blunt than that of the production elevators, beveled trailing edges, a geared balancing tab with a linkage ratio of -0.33, and a control-system mechanical advantage that gave stick forces 22 percent less than that of the production arrangement for a given hinge moment. For the production elevators with the standard control system and a 5-pound bobweight the variation in maneuvering stick forces over the operating center-of-gravity range was 5 to 24 pounds per g. A set of elevators was tested that provided further reduction in the value of variation of elevator hinge-moment coefficient with elevator deflection, in an effort to obtain stick forces within the desired limits of 3 to 8 pounds per g over the operating center-of-gravity range. These elevators in conjunction with an 8-pound bobweight were found to provide a stick-force variation with center-of-gravity position in steady turns of about this magnitude, but the control was considered very objectionable by the pilot because it resulted in involuntary overcontrol during take-offs and rapid elevator movements. Because of this consideration no reduction in the variation of maneuvering forces with center-of-gravity position below that given by the improved arrangement mentioned previously was possible.[23]

A summarization of the Helldiver wing-tip slot flight research studies was presented by Reeder and engineer M.D. White in another official NACA Memorandum Report:

Flight tests have been conducted on an SB2C-1 airplane to determine the effects of the wing-tip slots on the flight characteristics of the airplane. The results indicate that in stalls in all flight conditions with the slots closed and covered with doped fabric and the wing leading edge smoothed, slightly higher values of the maximum normal-force coefficient were obtained than with the production arrangement where the slots were opened when the landing gear was extended. The production slot arrangement did reduce the maximum rolling velocities and accelerations experienced in the stall roll-off. The aileron control characteristics and the longitudinal stability of the airplane at low speeds were unaffected by the slot arrangement and it appears that, neglecting the effect of the difference in weight due to the slots, the take-off performance will also be unaffected by the slot arrangement.[24]

A Curtiss SB2C Helldiver awaits flight research studies at Langley. *NASA Langley Research Center via Don Loving Collection.*

Frontal view of the Helldiver awaiting flight research studies at Langley. *NASA Langley Research Center via Don Loving Collection.*

A Curtiss SB2C-1 Helldiver on display at Langley in 1943.

Frontal view of the SB2C-1 awaiting control system and maneuverability flight research studies at Langley in 1943. *NASA Langley Research Center via Don Loving Collection.*

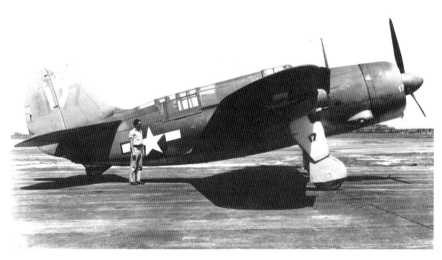

Another Curtiss SB2C-1 Helldiver awaits control system and maneuverability flight research studies at Langley in 1943. The Helldiver went on to serve as an excellent replacement for the venerable Douglas SBD Dauntless. *NASA Langley Research Center via Larry Loftin Collection.*

A Curtiss SB2C-4 Helldiver awaits flight testing at Langley in January 1945. *NASA Langley Research Center via Don Loving Collection.*

A Douglas SBD-5 Dauntless awaits handling and performance flight research studies at Langley in late 1944.

Douglas SBD-5 Dauntless

In late 1944, NACA Langley performed handling and performance and pilot familiarization flight tests of an advanced version of the venerable Douglas SBD Dauntless dive bomber. The Dauntless earned the nickname "Slow but Deadly" in combat, its most significant contribution to Allied victory in the Pacific being the decimation of the vaunted Imperial Japanese Navy carrier fleet at the Battle of Midway. The Marine Corps also made use of this venerable veteran throughout much of the "Island Hopping" campaign in the Pacific.

TORPEDO BOMBERS

Grumman XTBF-1 Avenger

In early to mid-1942, NACA Langley performed flight research studies of the Grumman XTBF-1 Avenger prototype. These studies focused on the verification of data and modifications generated from NACA Langley

FST studies performed in 1942. Static longitudinal and directional stability flight research studies of the Avenger prototype were conducted at NACA Langley and revealed that the aircraft "had near neutral directional stability at small sideslip angles (0 to 5 degrees) caused by blanketing of the vertical tail by the disturbed flow behind the large greenhouse canopy. The use of a dorsal fin restored the directional stability at larger sideslip angles so that the characteristics were not considered dangerous."[25] NACA Langley pilots also performed Avenger test flights to attain pilot proficiency in torpedo bombers. The Avenger would go on to ravage Japanese shipping and German U-boats during the war.

In early to mid-1942, NACA Langley performed flight research studies on the Navy Grumman XTBF-1 Avenger prototype. These studies were aimed at the verification of data and modifications inspired by Full-Scale Wind Tunnel research studies performed earlier on the aircraft.

Frontal view of a General Motors TBM-1 Avenger at Langley for flight research studies late in the war. *NASA Langley Research Center via Don Loving Collection.*

LIGHT ATTACK BOMBERS

Douglas A-20 Havoc

In early 1942, NACA Langley conducted flight research studies of a production variant of the Douglas A-20 Havoc light attack bomber to verify modifications to the airplane's design that were made on suggestions recommended to Douglas resulting from NACA Langley FST engine cooling and aerodynamic performance wind-tunnel studies. The A-20 flight research studies verified the validity of the NACA wind-tunnel study-inspired modifications to the aircraft's design.

This Douglas A-20A Havoc arrived at Langley in 1941 for flight research studies. *NASA Langley Research Center via Don Loving Collection.*

Douglas A-26 Invader

In early 1944, NACA Langley performed flight research studies on a new light attack bomber, manufactured by Douglas and destined for U.S. Army Air Forces (USAAF) use, known as the A-26B Invader. These flight investigations focused on the reduction of aerodynamic drag of the airplane's engine nacelles. The studies resulted in modifications to the aircraft's design, which ultimately enhanced its performance. The Invader later made its combat debuts in both the European and Pacific Theaters and was highly effective in combat.

DeHavilland F-8 Mosquito

In late 1944, NACA Langley pilots had the opportunity to conduct stability, control and pilot familiarization evaluations of a British RAF DeHavilland F-8 Mosquito light bomber. During World War II, the Mosquito wrought havoc on German ground and maritime targets.

MEDIUM BOMBERS

Martin B-26 Marauder

In 1942, NACA Langley conducted performance and handling and pilot familiarization studies of the Martin B-26 Marauder medium bomber. These studies provided valuable data and information to aircrews flying Marauders in USAAF service in combat.

HEAVY BOMBERS

Consolidated B-24D Liberator

In mid-1943, NACA Langley performed performance and handling and pilot familiarization flight research studies on a Consolidated B-24D Liberator four-engine heavy bomber. The aircraft was also used for model bomb drop tests later in the war.

A Douglas A-26B Invader awaits drag-reduction flight research studies at Langley in early 1944. *NASA Langley Research Center via Larry Loftin Collection.*

On the forty-first anniversary of the Wright brothers' flight, December 17, 1944, the popular nationwide NBC *Army Hour* radio program was broadcast live from the LMAL, featuring reports from facilities and Langley personnel. In this photo, Mel Gough, head of the Flight Research Division, and Captain Peterson, *Army Hour* announcer, converse about the Langley research contributions for the P-51 and A-26 aircraft.

Side view of a British-built DeHavilland F-8 Mosquito at Langley in late 1944. *NASA Langley Research Center via Don Loving Collection.*

Frontal view of the Mosquito at Langley in late 1944.

A Martin B-26 Marauder used in flight research studies at Langley in 1942. *NASA Langley Research Center via Don Loving Collection.*

This B-26 experienced a landing mishap at Langley on August 15, 1942. *NASA Langley Research Center via Don Loving Collection.*

A Consolidated B-24D Liberator used in flight research studies at Langley in 1943. *NASA Langley Research Center via Don Loving Collection.*

A Consolidated B-24D Liberator used in performance and handling flight research studies at Langley in 1943. *NASA Langley Research Center via Don Loving Collection.*

An Army Consolidated B-24D Liberator, flown from Langley Field, ditches in the James River in 1944. This flight test project was performed jointly between the NACA and the Army Air Force to determine how to better optimize the chances for survival of a water impact in heavy bombers. Note the James River Bridge visible in the background.

Rescue and salvage crews arrive at the scene of the successful ditching of an Army B-24D Liberator in the James River in 1944.

A huge crane positioned on a barge lifts the B-24D out of the James River following a successful ditching. Note the damage to the aircraft's belly.

Interestingly, NACA Langley and the Army Air Forces jointly performed a unique flight test program in 1944 that significantly benefitted the Allied war effort. An army Consolidated Liberator performed a flight from Langley Field in which the aircraft was intentionally ditched in the James River. This test flight yielded a plethora of data for Allied heavy bomber aircrews and aircraft manufacturers concerning ways in which aircrews could best survive water impacts in large four-engine heavy bombers. During this study, the impact force on the airplane's bomb bay doors and aircraft structural components was determined. This data was shared with aircraft designers and combat operational squadrons in both the European and Pacific Theaters. The flight research study ultimately saved a tremendous number of Allied aircrew lives.

Boeing B-17G Flying Fortress

In 1945, NACA Langley conducted radar bombing flight research studies using a Boeing B-17G Flying Fortress heavy bomber in concert with the USAAF at Langley Field. In addition, the aircraft was utilized as a bomb model drop mother ship in transonic research studies.

Top: A Boeing B-17G Flying Fortress used for radar bombing experiments and mother ship duty for "free-fall" bomb model drop transonic research studies in 1945.

Bottom: A free-fall bomb drop model attached to the underwing pylon of the B-17G mother ship at NACA Langley in 1945. *NASA Langley Research Center via Larry Loftin Collection.*

Boeing B-29 Superfortress

In early 1945, NACA Langley acquired two Boeing B-29 Superfortress four-engine heavy bombers for flight research purposes. One aircraft was utilized in handling and performance characteristics flight research, while the other aircraft was used as a mother ship for "free-fall" bomb model drop transonic research studies. During the B-29 "free-fall" studies, a "free-fall" drop bomb model was dropped from an underwing pylon positioned close to the aircraft fuselage at a high altitude to study its aerodynamics at speeds in excess of Mach 1 via radar monitoring and telemetering. The majority of these test flights were conducted above Langley's Plum Tree Island bombing range. The flight tests yielded data deemed to be "critical," since wind tunnels at the time lacked transonic or supersonic speed run capability.

Above: A Boeing B-29 Superfortress used in flight research studies at Langley. *NASA Langley Research Center via Don Loving Collection.*

Opposite, top: Side view of a B-29B used as a bomb drop model mother ship at NACA Langley in 1945. *NASA Langley Research Center via Don Loving Collection.*

Opposite, middle: A B-29 bomb drop model mother ship in flight over the waters near NACA Langley in 1945.

Opposite, bottom: A free-fall bomb drop model attached to the underwing pylon of a B-29 mother ship at Langley. *NASA Langley Research Center via Larry Loftin Collection.*

SEAPLANES AND FLYING BOATS

uring World War II, NACA Langley conducted flight research studies of the land version of one late-war seaplane, the Curtiss SC Seahawk, and one flying boat, the Consolidated PBY-5A Catalina. The Seahawk flight research studies were aimed at verifying engine air-cooling FST wind-tunnel study results, while the Catalina studies were aimed at confirming the validity of modifications to the aircraft's design resulting from NACA Langley tow tank research.

Seaplanes

Curtiss SC Seahawk (Land Version)

In late 1944 and 1945, the NACA Langley Flight Research Division performed flight research studies of a Curtiss SC Seahawk (land version) seaplane. The Seahawk was designed as a replacement for the venerable Vought OS2U Kingfisher seaplane flown by the Navy and Marine Corps as an observation/patrol aircraft. At Langley, a land version of the Seahawk was test-flown and evaluated in performance and handling characteristics studies as well as flight research studies aimed at the verification and validation of modifications to the aircraft's design brought about by NACA Langley Seahawk engine air-cooling FST studies. The Seahawk went on to serve as an excellent replacement for the Kingfisher in the latter years of the war.

A land-version Curtiss SC-1 Seahawk seaplane awaits flight testing at NACA Langley. *NASA Langley Research Center via Don Loving Collection.*

FLYING BOATS

A Sikorsky JRS-1 flying boat awaits flight research studies at NACA Langley. *NASA Langley Research Center via Don Loving Collection.*

A Grumman JRF-5 Goose flying boat awaits flight research studies at NACA Langley. *NASA Langley Research Center via Don Loving Collection.*

Consolidated PBY-5A Catalina

In 1945, NACA Langley test-flew and evaluated a Consolidated PBY-5A in verification and validation studies designed to assess the effects of modifications to the flying boat's hull as well as spray characteristics produced from model tests in Langley's Tow Tank No. 1 facility. These studies led to

A Consolidated PBY-5A Catalina flying boat awaits flight testing at NACA Langley in 1945. *NASA Langley Research Center via Larry Loftin Collection.*

a reduction in and solution to problems experienced with spray washing onto the windshield and engine parts while operating at sea. The Catalina went on to achieve "legendary" status during World War II and provided the Navy with critical search and rescue, reconnaissance and maritime patrol and anti-submarine mission capabilities.

15

TRANSPORTS

NACA Langley conducted flight research studies of leading-edge transports during World War II that represented the epitome of transport aircraft technology at the time. Some of these studies even benefited the design of high-altitude heavy bombers during the latter years of the war.

A Lockheed 12 transport awaits flight testing at NACA Langley in 1943. *NASA Langley Research Center via Don Loving Collection.*

DOUGLAS C-39

In 1940, NACA Langley performed performance and handling characteristics flight research studies of a Douglas C-39, the predecessor of the famous USAAF C-47 Skytrain and U.S. Navy R4D Gooney Bird. Langley pilots found this aircraft, much like its civilian DC-3 variant, to be a superb transport, and they immediately began to familiarize themselves with piloting it to maintain their proficiency levels. The Skytrain went on to serve the USAAF well as a transport for paratroopers, most notably during the D-Day invasion of Normandy in Nazi-occupied France. The Gooney Bird went on to serve as an excellent transport for the Navy and Marine Corps during the war.

A Douglas C-39, precursor to the famous Army C-47 Skytrain and Navy R4D Gooney Bird, awaits flight research studies at NACA Langley in 1940. *NASA Langley Research Center via Don Loving Collection.*

LOCKHEED XC-35

In 1943, NACA Langley initiated flight research studies of the revolutionary Lockheed XC-35, an experimental transport aircraft built for the Army to perform high-altitude research. The airplane was the first twin-engine aircraft in the world to use a pressurized cabin. The airplane also became NACA Langley's first "storm-chaser" aircraft, with Langley pilots deliberately flying the aircraft into severe thunderstorms for research purposes.

During World War II, NACA Langley conducted XC-35 flight studies aimed at studying the formation of aircraft contrails at high altitudes and how to reduce their appearance. Armed with this knowledge, American high-altitude heavy bomber crews were able to devise combat flight routines that prevented their bombers from being detected by enemy fighter pilots and anti-aircraft crews. The Langley XC-35 contrail formation flight research studies proved to significantly benefit American high-altitude heavy bomber aircrews operating their aircraft in the European combat theater.

Also during World War II, NACA Langley modified the XC-35 to operate with turbo-supercharged engines, enabling the aircraft to provide aircraft industry and military planners with valuable data regarding high-altitude flight and pressurized cabins.

The revolutionary Lockheed XC-35 awaits flight research studies at NACA Langley.

ROTORCRAFT

Duri ng World War II, NACA Langley gained the distinction of being the first government laboratory to conduct flight research studies of the first true helicopter in the world, the Sikorsky YR-4B/HNS-1 Hoverfly. The Langley Hoverfly flight research findings ultimately benefited Hoverfly service pilots and aircrews, helping them to fly the helicopter effectively and safely when rescuing downed Allied airmen in the Pacific in 1945.

Sikorsky YR-4B/HNS-1 Hoverfly

In 1944, NACA Langley assigned Jack Reeder to the Coast Guard Station at Floyd Bennett airport in Brooklyn, New York, to undergo training for a unique series of test flights of the world's first practical helicopter, the Sikorsky YR-4B (Army variant) or HNS-1 (Navy variant). Aviation pioneer Igor Sikorsky was the designer of the YR-4B/HNS-1 "Hoverfly." This design utilized primarily a single rotor and became the standard helicopter design adopted the world over.

The first test flight studies of the Navy HNS-1 at NACA Langley were performed by Jack Reeder in March 1945. Tests of the Army version (YR-4B) in the Langley FST had already been performed in October 1944 and led to a determination of the helicopter's aerodynamic behavior and rotor characteristics. Reeder worked closely with engineer Frederick B. Gustafson during the "Hoverfly" flight research program. Gustafson had already risen to "legend" status among the rotorcraft community. The two men summarized some of the issues encountered when flying helicopters in a NACA report published in 1954:

> It has been suggested in the past that flying a helicopter is a new and difficult art. In its present stage of development, the helicopter is different and more difficult to fly than most airplanes. The difficulty seems to arise from three sources: the helicopter has one additional control (collective pitch) to be operated; the power controls (collective pitch and throttle) must be used almost continuously in conjunction with flight controls during operations near the ground, chiefly because of the rapid variation of power required with airspeed in the speed range normally used in these operations; and, the helicopter has undesirable stability characteristics in forward flight which would not be acceptable in an airplane. Hovering flight also introduces a new and unique problem which is, however, somewhat analogous to formation flying with airplanes.
>
> The NACA has long been vitally interested in stability and control problems and in setting up requirements for the satisfactory stability and control characteristics for airplanes. We are now in the process of extending this work to cover the case of the helicopter. It is recognized that airplane requirements may not be applicable to helicopters in a specific manner but, nevertheless, the underlying reason for setting up the requirements applies to both airplane and helicopter. We feel that sooner or later the helicopter is going to have to meet requirements parallel to those for the airplane in order to reach its potential capabilities.[26]

The HNS-1 flight tests were aimed at determining the rotor performance, including identifying which rotor blades and which rotor blade configurations performed most efficiently. In addition, the helicopter's stability and control characteristics were also studied.

> During the course of the performance tests, considerable flying was done at relatively high speeds, approaching the limits imposed by blade stalling. It was found quite difficult to hold steady conditions because of a strong tendency of the machine to diverge in pitch, creating the impression of balancing on a ball. This characteristic seemed far more pronounced with some of the rotors tested than with others, but was always troublesome.

Upward pitching was most troublesome as it frequently precipitated or intensified stalling, which added to the difficulties because it increased the tendency to pitch up and was accompanied by rather violent periodic stick forces and vibration. The forward displacement of the control from trim necessary to check some of these pitching motions suggested that a short delay in applying corrective control would allow a maneuver severe enough that control would be lost. Although there seemed ample control to stop downward pitching, an uncomfortable amount of forward control was again required in order to check the subsequent upward pitching. These characteristics suggested a pronounced type of instability.

The tendency to depart from the trim speed and the necessity of applying appreciable control deflection against a pitching maneuver involving acceleration, initiated either by control or by external disturbances, is apparent throughout the speed range normally used in forward flight. It becomes much less pronounced, however, at the lower speeds.

Shortly after the embryo pilot experiences forward flight, he is impressed with the necessity for having to constantly fly the helicopter. At first thought the reasons for this situation are not clear. It is common knowledge that a flapping rotor tilts to the rear if speed is increased, thus tending to cause the machine to return to the original speed. Wind-tunnel tests of the YR-4B fuselage have shown it to be unstable, but this instability is evidently outweighed by the rotor stability just discussed, in as much as measurements of stick position have shown that the stick does move forward to trim at increasing steady speeds. Furthermore, observation and measurements have indicated that the static stick-force gradient with respect to speed is small, but has been either unstable, neutral, or stable, depending upon the pitching moments of the particular blades and upon the bungee configuration, without greatly altering the pilot's overall impression of instability. The source of the difficulty, therefore, cannot be either stick-fixed or stick-free instability with speed.

The somewhat obvious conclusion is that the pilot's impressions are a result of the helicopter's instability with angle of attack. There are at least two logical sources for its instability with angle of attack. The first results from the flapping of the rotor. If the helicopter rotor is subjected to an angle-of-attack change in forward flight, then for constant rpm the advancing blades are subjected to a greater upward accelerating force than the retreating blades because the product of angle-of-attack change and velocity squared is greater on the advancing side. The resulting flapping motion will then tilt the disk in the direction of the initial change, which results in an unstable moment. *This effect is a function of the tip-speed ratio and becomes more pronounced at higher speeds. The second source is the unstable fuselage.*

It may be well to point out here that airplanes can and do exhibit instability with angle of attack at times, but this condition is recognized as unsatisfactory and is generally prevented by keeping the center of gravity sufficiently well forward.[27]

Finally, Reeder evaluated the helicopter's hovering characteristics.

Hovering, of course, precedes and follows all forward flight and is the outstanding reason for the existence of helicopter types. We feel, however, that at present the problems associated with hovering in this particular type are more indefinite than in forward flight, that they tend to disappear with a little flight practice, and that they don't affect its general utility to the extent that limitations on night and instrument flying do.[28]

Jack Reeder performs a test flight in the Sikorsky HNS-1 Hoverfly at NACA Langley in March 1945. Reeder was the NACA/NASA's first helicopter pilot.

The Langley "Hoverfly" wind-tunnel and flight research programs led to important modifications to the design of the rotorcraft, which enabled it to excel in the search and rescue (SAR) role during the final year of the war. Moreover, the NACA Langley "Hoverfly" flight research program data were ultimately incorporated in the military flight qualities specifications for helicopters.

PART III

· · · · · · · · · · · · · · · · · ·

SUMMARY

World War II aeronautical research at NACA Langley decidedly helped the Allies win the war. NACA Langley's wind-tunnel research resulted in performance-enhancing modifications to military aircraft designs that proved to be crucial to Allied victory. Langley's flight research studies of Allied military aircraft during the war led to modifications of their designs that enhanced their capabilities, enabling them to perform better and outclass the enemy in combat. During the war, the NACA expanded tremendously, blossoming from one research lab, the LMAL, to three research labs, the other two being the Ames Aeronautical Laboratory in Mountain View, California, and the Aircraft Engine Research Laboratory in Cleveland, Ohio. "Employment peaked at 6,077 employees in 1945 and the budget that same year was almost $41 million."[29] Through its aeronautical research, NACA Langley not only helped the Allies win World War II but also helped to perfect the technologies that led the way to the future of military aviation.

NOTES

Chapter 2

1. George W. Gray, *Frontiers of Flight: The Story of NACA Research* (New York: Alfred A. Knopf, 1945), 36–37.
2. D.D. Baals and W.R. Corliss, *Wind Tunnels of NASA* (Washington, DC: National Aeronautics and Space Administration, 1981), 21.

Chapter 4

3. John P. Reeder and William J. Biebel, *Memorandum Report for Bureau of Aeronautics, Navy Department, Tests of Grumman XTBF-1 Airplane in the NACA Full-Scale Tunnel* (Langley Field, VA: National Advisory Committee for Aeronautics, Langley Memorial Aeronautical Laboratory, October 21, 1942), 16–17.
4. John P. Reeder and G. Merritt Preston, *Memorandum Report for the Army Air Corps Full-Scale Wind Tunnel Tests of the General Motors Aerial Torpedo* (Langley Field, VA: National Advisory Committee for Aeronautics, Langley Memorial Aeronautical Laboratory, October 29, 1941), 1, 8.
5. Interview with John P. Reeder, March 21, 1994, Newport News, Virginia.
6. John P. Reeder and Gerald W. Brewer, *Memorandum Report for Bureau of Aeronautics, Navy Department, NACA Full-Scale Wind-Tunnel Tests of Vought Sikorsky V-173 Airplane* (Langley Field, VA: National Advisory Committee

for Aeronautics, Langley Memorial Aeronautical Laboratory, April 28, 1941), 23–24.

Chapter 9

7. Gray, *Frontiers of Flight*, 74–75.

Chapter 12

8. C.H. Dearborn, Abe Silverstein and J.P. Reeder, *Army Air Corps Material Division, War Department Test of XP-40 Airplane in NACA Full-Scale Tunnel* (Langley Field, VA: National Advisory Committee for Aeronautics, Langley Memorial Aeronautical Laboratory, May 16, 1939), 17.

9. W. Hewitt Phillips, *Journey in Aeronautical Research: A Career at NASA Langley Research Center, Monographs in Aerospace History, Number 12* (Washington, DC: NASA History Office, Office of Policy and Plans, NASA Headquarters, November 1998), 24.

10. Ibid.

11. Laurence K. Loftin Jr., "A Research Pilot's World as Seen from the Cockpit of a NASA Engineer-Pilot," unpublished manuscript, July 1986, chapter 3, 14–15.

12. Interview with Todd Hodges, June 16, 2006, Yorktown, Virginia.

13. Christopher C. Kraft Jr., Fabian R. Goranson and John P. Reeder, *National Advisory Committee for Aeronautics (Technical Note 2899): Measurements of Flying Qualities of an F-47D-30 Airplane to Determine Longitudinal Stability and Control and Stalling Characteristics* (Langley, VA: Langley Aeronautical Laboratory, February 1953, 1.

14. *Virginia Aviation*, "Jack Reeder Retires from NASA-Langley" 14 (October–December 1980), Commonwealth of Virginia Department of Aviation, 1.

15. Ibid.

16. Christopher C. Kraft Jr. and J.P. Reeder, *National Advisory Committee for Aeronautics Research Memorandum for the Air Material Command, U.S. Air Force (NACA RM No. SL8B24): Measurements of the Longitudinal Stability and Control and Stalling Characteristics of a North American P-51H Airplane (AFF NO. 4-64164)* (Langley Field, VA: National Advisory Committee for Aeronautics Langley Memorial Aeronautical Laboratory, no date), 1 and 9.

17. Loftin, "Research Pilot's World," chapter 5, 6.

18. Walter C. Williams and John P. Reeder, *National Advisory Committee for Aeronautics Memorandum Report for the Bureau of Aeronautics, Navy Department: Flight Measurements of the Flying Qualities of an F6F-3 Airplane (BUAER NO. 04776) I—Longitudinal Stability and Control* (Langley Field, VA: National Advisory Committee for Aeronautics Langley Memorial Aeronautical Laboratory, February 13, 1945), 1.

19. Ibid., 13–15.

20. Williams and Reeder, *National Advisory Committee for Aeronautics Memorandum Report III—Stalling Characteristics*, 4–5.

21. H.L. Crane and J.P. Reeder, *National Advisory Committee for Aeronautics Research Memorandum for the Bureau of Aeronautics, Navy Department: Flight Measurements of Lateral and Directional Stability and Control Characteristics of the Grumman F8F-1 Airplane (Ted No. NACA 2379); NACA RM No. L7L31* (Langley Field, VA: National Advisory Committee for Aeronautics Langley Memorial Aeronautical Laboratory, no date), 1.

22. Interview with W. Hewitt Phillips, June 13, 2006, Hampton, Virginia.

Chapter 13

23. Maurice D. White and John P. Reeder, *National Advisory Committee for Aeronautics Memorandum Report for the Bureau of Aeronautics, Navy Department: Flight Investigation of Modifications to Improve the Elevator Control-Force Characteristics of the Curtiss SB2C-1C Airplane in Maneuvers (TED NO. NACA 2333); NACA MR No. L5D04a* (Langley Field, VA: National Advisory Committee for Aeronautics Langley Memorial Aeronautical Laboratory, no date), 1–2.

24. M.D. White and J.P. Reeder, *National Advisory Committee for Aeronautics Memorandum Report for the Bureau of Aeronautics, Navy Department: Effect of Wing-Tip Slots on the Stalling and Aileron Control Characteristics of a Curtiss SB2C-1 Airplane (MR No. 14K13)* (Langley Field, VA: National Advisory Committee for Aeronautics Langley Memorial Aeronautical Laboratory, November 13, 1944), 1.

25. Phillips, *Journey in Aeronautical Research*, 33.

Chapter 16

26. J.P. Reeder and F.B. Gustafson, "Notes on the Flying Qualities of Helicopters," presented at the American Helicopter Society Meeting, April

22–24, 1948. National Advisory Committee for Aeronautics, Washington and Langley Aeronautical Laboratory, Langley Field, Virginia, April 22, 1948, 1.

27. Ibid., 2–4.

28. Ibid., 7.

Part III

29. NASA Langley Research Center, "NASA Facts: World War II and the National Advisory Committee for Aeronautics: U.S. Aviation Research Helped Speed Victory," Hampton, Virginia, July 1995, 1.

ABOUT THE AUTHOR

M ark A. Chambers works as a technical writer for Huntington Ingalls Industries / Newport News Shipbuilding in Newport News, Virginia. He is the author of six Arcadia Publishing titles: *Flight Research at NASA Langley Research Center*, *Naval Air Station Patuxent River*, *NASA Kennedy Space Center*, *Joint Base Langley-Eustis*, *Naval Air Station Norfolk* and *Naval Air Station Oceana Fleet Defenders*.

Visit us at
www.historypress.com
··